INTRODUCTION

The term 'Mechanized Warfare' originated in the First World War and has remained in military parlance ever since. In general, it has come to refer to the tank, the weapon that broke the trench stalemate on the Western Front, and the armoured car, which became increasingly heavier and better armed to a point where it could exploit the breaches made in enemy defences by the tank and carry out attacks behind enemy lines. It was these armoured vehicles that captured the imagination of the public, to the detriment of a host of other armoured vehicles – trucks, tractors, cars and gun carriers – which became vital to the support of the armies in the field.

The main problem with such support vehicles was that they relied on reasonable roads to carry out their tasks, which meant that their usefulness was restricted and generally confined to the rear areas. It was left to horse-drawn transport to negotiate the more difficult terrain, completing the transit of supplies and ammunition to the frontlines. There was clearly a requirement for a more efficient method of transport, ideally a small, light, vehicle that had a respectable turn of speed and was fitted with tracks rather than wheels, enabling it to function in all types of terrain. Mounting a machine gun, it might also double as a light attack vehicle.

One man who was aware of such a requirement was Major Giffard Le Quesne Martel, a British military engineer and tank strategist who in 1916 had written a paper suggesting the formation of an army composed entirely of armoured vehicles. In 1925, in his garage, he built a one-man mini-tank – a Tankette – powered by a car engine and capable of a speed of 15 miles per hour. A demonstration to the War Office resulted in a contract being issued to Morris Commercial Motors to build four test vehicles in 1926 and also awakened the interest of a number of commercial motor manufacturing firms, one of which was Carden-Loyd Tractors Ltd. In 1927 this company, founded by John V. Carden and

Vivian Graham Loyd in the early 1920s, built a one-man Tankette, followed by several two-man vehicles. Trials proved to be an instant success and production of the vehicles for both the home and export markets began in 1927, continuing when Carden-Loyd was taken over by Vickers-Armstrongs in 1928. Carden himself was employed by Vickers as the technical director, and together with Loyd continued to develop the Tankette.

The whole purpose of the Tankette was the rapid deployment of troops armed with machine guns, which were not intended

The definitive version of the Carden Loyd Tankette was the Mk VI, seen here armed with a Vickers 0.303 medium machine gun. (Vickers)

The Carden Loyd Tankette enjoyed huge export success, being employed by the armies of nine nations as well as the British Army. (Vickers)

Among other light tank designs that appeared in the 1920s was this 6-ton vehicle, which was ordered from the Royal Ordnance Factory in 1925 and was originally intended to be a three-man tank. Trials showed that this rather clumsy vehicle was no more acceptable as a machine gun carrier than it was as a light tank. (Vickers)

A lineup of Vickers Carden Loyd Utility Light Tractors (Vickers)

to be fired from the vehicle itself, although a tripod mounting for a machine gun was attached to the front of the hull. The Tankettes could also be used to tow light howitzers. Exports were a success, the Tankette being acquired by Canada, Chile, Czechoslovakia, France, India, Italy, Japan, Poland and the USSR, who used it to develop their own T-27 design. The definitive version, Mk VI, and earlier versions were also used by the British Army, which took delivery of 270 examples.

As well as light tanks, Carden and Loyd also developed a series of light artillery tractors and carriers, one of which was the Dragon artillery tractor, designed to tow a standard 18-pounder gun. The Dragon provided seating for the gun crew (up to ten men) and had provision for 64 rounds of field gun ammunition and battery equipment. The Dragon Mk I, which entered service with the British Army in 1924, was powered by a 60hp Leyland four-cylinder engine, which gave it a top road speed of 12mph. It was followed in 1926 by the Dragon Mk II, which had a fully enclosed superstructure and was fitted with an Armstrong Siddeley 82hp V8 engine. Although its road speed of 16mph was an improvement over that of the Mk I, its hauling capability proved to be less, so improvements to the engine drive resulted in the Mk II, which could carry eleven men and 128 rounds of ammunition.

The problem with the Dragon tractors was that they were expensive and over-complicated, so in 1934 Vickers launched a new light tracked vehicle, the D50, which could be used either to tow a light field gun or carry a heavy Vickers machine gun. The D50 was very simple in design, with a two-man compartment at the front and bench seats running lengthways along the track guards at the rear to accommodate the rest of the crew. The engine, located centrally in the body, was a standard Ford V-8 commercial motor, linked by a four-speed and reverse gearbox to a standard Ford truck rear axle at the back.

John Carden, meanwhile, had inherited the Irish baronetage of Tempelmore in 1931, and was now Sir John. His elevation to the nobility was tragically cut short on 10 September 1935, when the Savoia-Marchetti S.73 airliner of the Belgian airline SABENA, in which he was flying as a passenger from Brussels to Croydon, crashed near Tatsfield in Surrey with the loss of all thirteen on board. After this accident Vivian Loyd, who had always worked in Carden's shadow, experienced increasingly strained relations with Vickers, and in 1938 he left the firm and founded his own company, producing a successful and cheap light tracked artillery tractor, the Loyd Carrier. Total production of this vehicle reached 26,000.

Although the D50 was not accepted for service with the British Army, in 1935 Vickers-Armstrongs offered a new design to the War Office. A prototype, known as an Experimental Armoured Machine Gun Carrier, underwent trials at the Mechanisation Experimental Establishment (MEE) Farnborough and as a result a contract was issued to Vickers-Armstrongs in April 1936 for thirteen more vehicles under the designation Carrier, Machine Gun, No 1 Mk 1. Some of these were adapted to different roles, the first being the Carrier Machine Gun No 2 Mk 1. Production of this vehicle ran to 1,000 units.

Another was the Armoured General Scout Vehicle, armed with a Bren light machine gun in place of the Vickers and a Boys anti-tank gun and fitted with wireless equipment. The Boys gun, more correctly designated Rifle, Boys, Anti-Tank .55in, was created by Captain Henry C. Boys, a designer at the Royal Small Arms Factory, Enfield. It was originally given the name Stanchion, but was renamed after its designer when Captain Boys died a few days before the weapon was approved for service in November 1937.

Other experimental designs included a Mortar Carrier, intended to carry a 3-inch mortar, and another designed to mount a 2-pounder anti-tank gun behind a large shield mounted above the engine. None of these variants went into production, but they paved the way for a single vehicle capable of fulfilling a variety of roles: in other words, a Universal Carrier.

Design & Development

The path that would eventually lead to the deployment of a true all-round universal vehicle was laid in 1937, when the British Army's Machine Gun Carriers were adapted to take a new light machine gun recently issued to infantry units. This was the Bren, a license-produced version of the Czech ZGB 33 weapon. The name Bren was derived from Brno, the town in Moravia where the gun was manufactured, and Enfield, where it was produced by the British Royal Small Arms Factory.

Designed by Vaclav Holek, the Bren was a highly accurate weapon with an effective firing range of 600yd (550m) and a maximum range of 1850yd (1,690m). It used 0.303 ammunition, same as that used by the standard British bolt-action Lee-Enfield rifle, and had a muzzle velocity of 2440ft/sec (743.7m/sec). The Bren was a gas-operated weapon, the propellant gases venting from a port towards the muzzle end of the barrel through a regulator with four quick-adjustment apertures of different sizes, intended to tailor the gas volume to different ambient temperatures (smallest flow at high temperature, e.g. summer desert, largest at low temperature, e.g. winter Arctic). The vented gas drove a piston which in turn actuated the breech block. Each gun came with a spare barrel that could be quickly changed when the barrel became hot during sustained fire. To change barrels, the release catch in front of the magazine was rotated to unlock the barrel. The carrying handle above the barrel was used to grip and remove the hot barrel without burning the hands.

The Bren was magazine-fed, which slowed its rate of fire and required more frequent reloading than British belt-fed machine guns such as the Vickers. The slower rate of fire prevented more rapid overheating of the Bren's air-cooled barrel, and the Bren was much lighter than belt-fed machine guns which typically had cooling jackets, often liquid filled. The magazines also prevented the ammunition from getting dirty, which was more of a problem with the Vickers with its 250-round canvas belts. The sights were offset to the left, to avoid the magazine on the top of the weapon. The position of the sights meant that the Bren could be fired only from the right shoulder. The Bren required a two-man crew, the gunner and his assistant. It was the ideal weapon for

The Boys 0.55in anti-tank rifle was effective against light-skinned vehicles, but useless against heavier armour. It was later replaced by the PIAT (Projector, Infantry, Anti-Tank). (Wikipedia)

The Czech-designed Bren light machine gun was an extremely effective and very accurate weapon. (IWM)

the new generation of light tracked infantry support vehicles.

Production of the carrier began in 1934 and it remained in service (in various armies) until 1960. In that time 113,000 vehicles had been produced in the United Kingdom and abroad. British production, undertaken initially by Aveling and Porter, Bedford Vehicles, Morris Motors Ltd, the Sentinel Waggon Works and the Thorneycroft Company, totalled some 57,000 units. The Ford Motor Company of Canada manufactured a further 29,000 vehicles, known as Ford C01 UC Universal Carriers, while 20,000 were built in the United States, about 5,000 in Australia and 1,300 in New Zealand.

The popular name Bren Gun Carrier stuck even when production switched to the definitive Universal Carrier in April 1939, production contracts for the first 2,275 vehicles being issued to Aveling-Barford,

Ford, Sentinel, Nuffield, Thorneycroft and Wolseley Motors.

By the time the Bren Gun Carrier entered service the British Army had become experienced in the theory of armoured manoeuvre, although the practice left much to be desired. What was intended to be a balanced force incorporating all types of armoured vehicle, known as the Experimental Mechanized Force (EMF), had been established at Tidworth Camp on Salisbury Plain in May 1927, and the Carden Loyd Machine Gun Carrier version of the tankette was used in the reconnaissance role from the beginning. In 1928 the EMF was renamed Armoured Force (AF), and in an exercise held later that year 280 vehicles of 15 types tested the force to its limits. At the end of the year further operations by the Armoured Force were suspended, the War Officer considering that there was no more to learn after the earlier manoeuvres, even though General George Milne, Chief of the Imperial General Staff, wanted further time to set up an experimental brigade with a battalion of light tanks and tankettes plus a battalion of infantry. An experimental Tank Brigade was in fact established in 1931 with three battalions of mixed medium and light tanks and a battalion of Carden Loyd machine gun carriers operating as light tanks for reconnaissance but with no supporting arms.

When the Tank Brigade began to train as a cohesive unit, it had four battalions, three with a combination of medium tanks and tankettes and a light tank battalion with three companies of light tanks and tankettes. Each medium company had an HQ section of four medium tanks and three mixed companies with a command tank, a section of seven tankettes or light tanks, one section of five medium tanks and a section of two tanks for close support, theoretically carrying guns capable of firing high explosive shells; no tanks were armed like this and Vickers medium tanks were substituted instead. During manoeuvres conducted in the mid-1930s the light tracked vehicles performed extremely well, and when the tankettes were replaced by Bren Gun Carriers in the late 1930s there was every expectation that the new arrivals would be equally as successful.

At this stage, no official assessment had been made of the Blitzkrieg tactics being developed by the newly created German Army, nor was much notice being taken of the new generation of German armoured fighting vehicles whose crews were sharpening their skills on the battlefields of Spain.

Vickers Medium Mk I tanks on manoeuvres with the Experimental Mechanized Force, 1927. (Vickers)

Bren Gun Carriers completed and awaiting delivery. (Vickers)

Personnel of the Welsh Guards inspecting one of their brand new Bren Gun Carriers shortly before the outbreak of the Second World War. (Vickers)

Carrier Variants

Carrier, Machine Gun, No 1 Mk I. Developed by Vickers in 1936, this vehicle became the prototype for subsequent machine gun and Bren Gun carriers. It was originally intended that the vehicle would carry an independent machine gun team operating a Vickers 0.303 medium machine gun, but then it was decided that the three-man crew could act as the gun team, operating internally or externally.

Carrier, General Purpose. This was an experimental vehicle which had its superstructure altered to form a projecting gunner's compartment at the front, but with a grooved rail around its top edge, in which was enclosed a four-wheeled mount for the Boys Anti-Tank Rifle. The operator of the rifle was able to traverse the gun through 180 degrees. It also was armed with a Bren LMG in the usual position. It was extensively tested in 1937, and although it did not go into production the modified design was incorporated in subsequent carriers.

Carrier, Machine Gun, No 2 Mk I. Deployed from late 1937, this production variant saw the earlier Vickers 0.303 replaced by the Bren LMG and/or the Boys AT rifle. The Carrier, Bren No 2 Mk II entered service in 1938 and although similar to its predecessor included some major alterations to the design. The main modifications were to the front armour where a gunner's projecting shield was introduced with a firing slot and hinged flap to assist the firing of the Boys AT Rifle, then being issued. Protective shields for the vision ports were provided. However the main significant change was to the front idler wheel, which was relocated to a higher position on the side hull. This produced a steeper track angle at the front and gave the vehicle its characteristic 'tail down' appearance. The higher idler also necessitated the forming of a curved section of front mudguard over this portion of track; this was to remain a standard feature in all subsequent carrier models.

Various marks of carrier were now being developed for specific roles. The first was the Carrier, Scout, Mk I, which entered service in 1938. Assigned to mechanized cavalry and light tank divisions, its function was to scout ahead and on the flanks of the main force and report on enemy movements by means of a No. 11 wireless set. The wireless operator, behind the driver, was protected by a high-sided armoured enclosure. The next model was the Carrier, Cavalry Mk I, which was designed to carry six men, three sitting

An early model of the Machine Gun Carrier Mk II, developed by Vickers in 1936 and mounting a Vickers 0.303 medium machine gun. (Vickers)

The driver of a Universal Carrier Mk I receiving instructions as he tows a truck clear of a ditch. (Source unknown)

The Wasp flamethrower variant of the Universal Carrier in action. (Wikimedia Commons)

The prototype of the unsuccessful Praying Mantis pictured in the Tank Museum, Bovington. (Tank Museum)

The Universal Carrier's box-like structure is well illustrated in this image of an example in a Polish military museum (Source unknown)

Australian made Universal Carriers, fresh off the production line. (Australian War Memorial)

on either side of the rear compartment facing the engine. This was not a popular vehicle as its occupants were not protected from enemy fire.

In 1939 the Carrier, Armoured, OP No.1, Mk I was issued to the Royal Artillery as a forward observation post. It contained a No.11 wireless set, a cable drum on the rear cover plate and an adjustable shutter over the gunner's firing slot to facilitate the use of binoculars. Based on the Carrier, Scout Mk I it was the first of a line of Observation Post (OP) carriers issued throughout the vehicle's production. The first ninety-five examples were built by Aveling-Barford, a large and internationally known company based in Grantham in Lincolnshire.

The Universal Carrier
In April 1939 the various roles and applications devised for the carrier so far converged at last under a single specification, and a single multi-purpose design known as the Universal Carrier came into being, initial contracts for 2,275 Mk I vehicles being issued to Aveling-Barford, Sentinel Waggon, Nuffield and Thorneycroft. Although the Universal Carrier underwent many modifications during its service, the basic design of the chassis remained unchanged. The Universal Carrier Mk II, introduced in 1942, was similar to the Mk I, but was equipped with a towing hitch. Some 11,000 Mk IIs were built by various British manufacturers.

A large number of variants based on the Mks I and II were developed. These included the Wasp, a flamethrower-equipped variant. The Mk I had a fixed flamethrower on the front of the vehicle fed from two fuel tanks with a combined capacity of 100 gallons. 1,000 were produced. In the Mk II, the flame projector was situated in the co-driver's position. A projected variant was the Mantis, an attempt to produce a low-silhouette vehicle that could still fire over obstacles. The idea arose out of the fighting in Normandy following the D-Day landings in June 1944, where the high banks and sunken lanes of the bocage presented serious obstacles to the Allied advance. A one-man design based on Carden Loyd suspension was not adopted, but the inventor was encouraged to design a two-man version. This version appeared in 1943 and was based on the Universal Carrier. The hull was replaced with an enclosed metal-box structure with enough room for a driver and a gunner lying prone. This box, pivoting from the rear, could be elevated. At the top end was a machine-gun turret (with two Bren guns). The intention was to drive the Mantis up to a wall or hedgerow, elevate the gun, and fire over the obstacle from a position of safety. It was rejected after trials later in 1944.

Australian Carriers

Carrier, Machine Gun, Local Pattern, No. 1: Also known as 'LP1 Carrier (Aust)'. Australian production vehicles were similar to the Bren Carrier but welded and incorporating some minor differences.

Universal Carrier MG, Local Pattern No. 2: Also known as 'LP2 Carrier (Aust). This was the Australian-built variant of the Universal Carrier, and was also produced in New Zealand. Used 1938–1939 Ford commercial axles; the 2A had 1940 Ford truck axles.

Two-pounder Anti-tank Gun Carrier (Aust) or Carrier, 2-pdr Tank Attack: A heavily modified and lengthened LP2 Carrier with a fully traversable quick-firing 2-pdr anti-tank gun mounted on a platform at the rear and the engine moved to the front left of the vehicle. Stowage was provided for 112 rounds of 2pdr ammunition. 200 were produced and used for training.

Three inch Mortar Carrier (Aust): This was a design based on the 2-pdr Carrier with a 3-inch mortar mounted in place of the 2 pounder. Designed to enable the mortar to have 360 degree traverse and to be fired either from the vehicle, or dismounted. 400 were produced and were ultimately sent as military aid to the Kuomintang (Chinese Nationalist) Army.

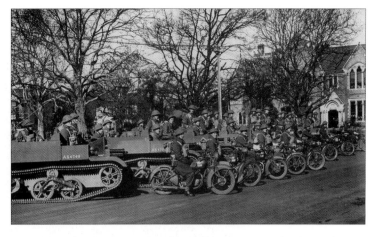

Universal Carriers and motorcycles of the 1st Battalion New Zealand Canterbury Regiment on display at Christchurch, 1942. (Australian War Memorial)

Australian Universal Carriers pictured on manoeuvres in the country's Northern Territory. (Australian War Memorial)

An Australian Bren Carrier LP2, restored and manned by re-enactors (Source unknown)

Right: An Australian-built Universal LP2A Carrier. Numbers of this variant were also produced in New Zealand. The principal manufacturer was South Australian Railways. (Shopland Collection)

A Universal Carrier Mk II, with the deep wading kit mounting pads welded around the upper hull, of the 1st Battalion Rocky Mountain Rangers, a Canadian reserve infantry regiment, on parade in Kamloops, British Columbia. (Borden Military Museum)

Canadian Carriers

Carrier, 2-pdr Equipped: Canadian modification to mount 2-pdr gun. 213 used for training. Wasp Mk IIC: Canadian version of the Wasp flamethrower variant. Windsor Carrier: Canadian development with a longer chassis extended 76cm and an additional wheel in the aft bogie.

This Canadian Universal Carrier bears the markings of the Royal Armoured Corps. (Borden Military Museum)

Above: A Canadian Universal Carrier pictured during a Second World War re-enactment in 2006 at the annual 'Thunder over Michigan' military event. The vehicle flies the pennant of the Nova Scotia Highlanders. (Via Kevin Fox)

The T-16 variant of the Universal Carrier, seen here in its Mk I guise with a protective covering in place, was a significantly improved vehicle based upon those built by Ford of Canada, manufactured under Lend-Lease by Ford in the United States from March 1943 to 1945. (Wikipedia)

United States Carriers

T-16: The Carrier, Universal, T16, Mark I. was a significantly improved vehicle based upon those built by Ford of Canada, manufactured under Lend-Lease by Ford in the United States from March 1943 to 1945. It was longer than the Universal with an extra road wheel on the rear bogie; making for a pair of full Horstmann dual-wheel suspension units per side, the engine was a Mercury-division 3.9 litre displacement Ford Flathead. Instead of a steering wheel controlling the combination brake/warp mechanism, the T-16 had track-brake steering operated by levers (two for each side). During the war, it was chiefly used by Canadian forces as an artillery tractor. After the war, it was used by mainly Argentine, Swiss and Netherlands forces.

Centre: A Ford-built T-16 Carrier shows its paces at a military vehicle display.

Right: T-16 carriers were much sought after by private collectors, like this example auctioned in Indiana.

The Universal Carrier in Detail

3D impression of a
Universal Carrier Mk II.

In the design of the Universal Carrier, and the series of light tracked carriers that led up to it, simplicity was the keyword, the vehicle being essentially a lightly armoured box on tracks with room for an engine and three crew members.

The driver and commander were seated side by side in the front of the vehicle, the driver on the right. The bulkhead immediately in front of the commander was extended forward to accommodate a Bren gun or other weapon, firing through a simple slit.

The first production model, the Carrier, Universal No 1 Mk I, set the pattern for all subsequent models, featuring a riveted hull with complete armour protection around the whole of the front and rear compartments. Most were provided with an angled hinged flap on the gunner's compartment side armour to assist the driver's view. The third crew member sat in the rear compartment behind the driver and his compartment had timber or rubber firing rests fixed to the armour edges. The now well proven carrier suspension, the Horstmann unit, with a double and single bogie wheel configuration each side, was used.

Direction control was effected by means of a steering wheel on the right which when rotated up to about 10 degrees off centre, warped or bowed the track so that a large radius turn could be accomplished without the use of brakes. At a greater angle of rotation, the steering wheel brought the braking system into play, halting the appropriate track and resulting in a tighter turning circle.

The opposite rear compartment was used for stowage and included a locker for crew belongings, brackets for Bren Gun tripod etc. Various models of the Mk I were produced which included minor upgrades from the Ford V8 65 bhp engine in the No 1 Mk I to the Ford V8 85 bhp engine in the Canadian built No 3 Mk I.

Behind the crew, in the centre of the vehicle, was the petrol engine, a Ford V8 developing 85hp at 3500rpm. The cylinders were arranged in two banks of four, at an angle of 45 degrees to the vertical. The suspension and running gear were based on that used by the Vickers light tank series, with the well-tried Horstmann suspension.

It was not until the Carrier, Universal No 1 Mk II came out in 1943 that alterations to the stowage and crew seating were made and improved upon. The vehicle also featured a welded waterproof hull. Again stowage types depended on the role of the vehicle. The re-positioning of the 2-inch

Detail of the Universal Carrier's track, suspension and wheels. (Tank Museum)

Fpr comparative purposes these thwo photographs show the suspension and running gear of the Australian LP2. Note the ribs on the spokes of the wheels.

mortar from the engine deck on the Mark I into the gunner's compartment on the Mark II was a major improvement, as was the re-siting of the crew locker to the rear of the carrier making more room for crew and/or equipment. Further stowage lockers were provided above each petrol tank.

The Carrier, Universal No 1 Mk III made its appearance soon afterwards and featured further stowage alterations, engine deck modifications and a new division plate between the front and rear compartments.

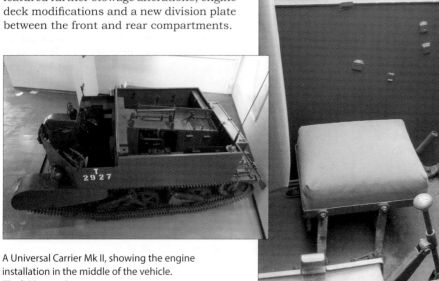

A Universal Carrier Mk II, showing the engine installation in the middle of the vehicle. (Tank Museum)

Right: The Universal Carrier driver's position, showing the vertical steering wheel. (Tank Museum)

The following eight 3D images depict a Universal Carrier Mk II. The recognition features of the Mk II have been indicated with an *.
Section compiled by Michael Roof

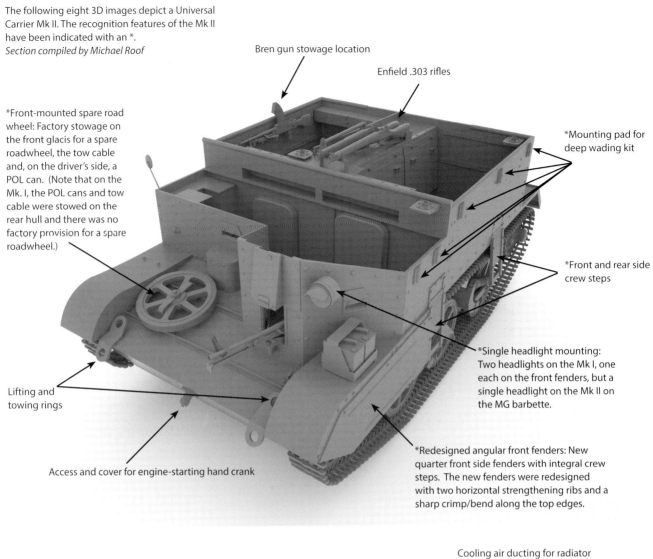

Bren gun stowage location

Enfield .303 rifles

*Mounting pad for deep wading kit

*Front-mounted spare road wheel: Factory stowage on the front glacis for a spare roadwheel, the tow cable and, on the driver's side, a POL can. (Note that on the Mk. I, the POL cans and tow cable were stowed on the rear hull and there was no factory provision for a spare roadwheel.)

*Front and rear side crew steps

Lifting and towing rings

*Single headlight mounting: Two headlights on the Mk I, one each on the front fenders, but a single headlight on the Mk II on the MG barbette.

Access and cover for engine-starting hand crank

*Redesigned angular front fenders: New quarter front side fenders with integral crew steps. The new fenders were redesigned with two horizontal strengthening ribs and a sharp crimp/bend along the top edges.

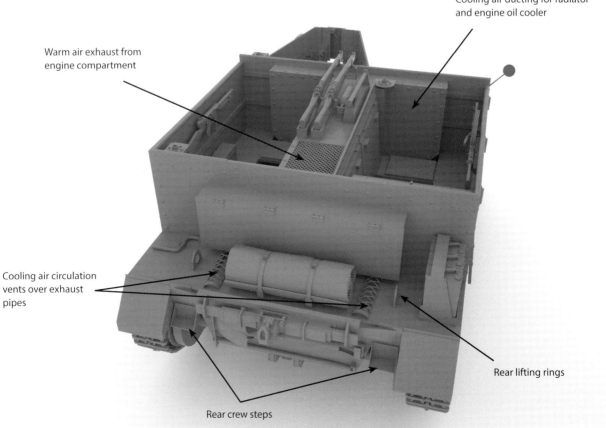

Cooling air ducting for radiator and engine oil cooler

Warm air exhaust from engine compartment

Cooling air circulation vents over exhaust pipes

Rear lifting rings

Rear crew steps

*Tubular upper edge guards on armoured compartment: Replacement of the Mk I rectangular cross-section wooden (rubbber) guards along the top edges of the side and rear armor with metal split-tubing guards.

*Redesigned, full-width rear stowage box: Revised rear stowage featuring a nearly full width storage box which replaces the multiple box arrangement of the Mk I

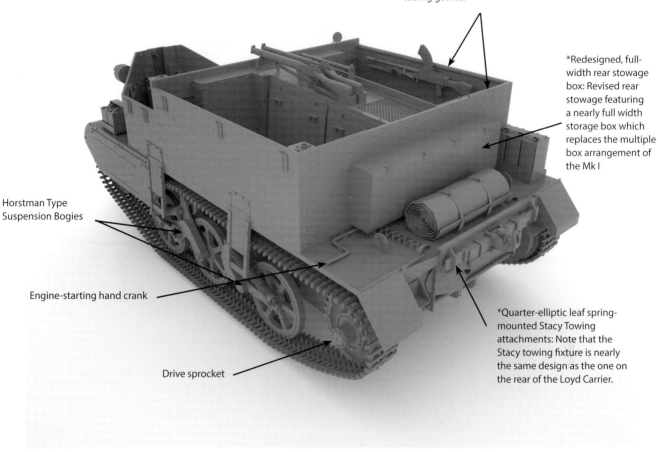

Horstman Type Suspension Bogies

Engine-starting hand crank

Drive sprocket

*Quarter-elliptic leaf spring-mounted Stacy Towing attachments: Note that the Stacy towing fixture is nearly the same design as the one on the rear of the Loyd Carrier.

Removeable panels (both sides) for engine access

Gunner/Commander position

Driver position

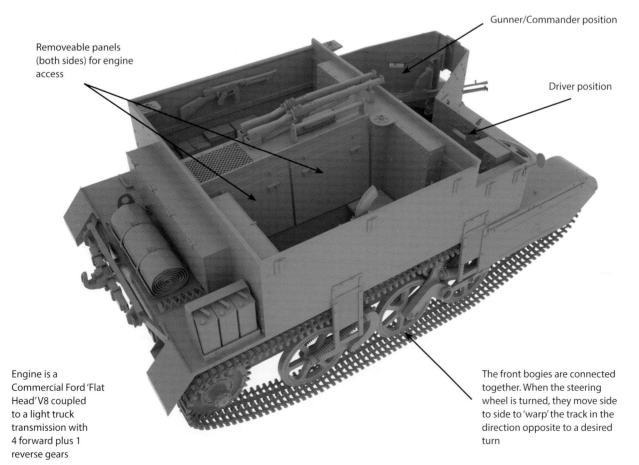

Engine is a Commercial Ford 'Flat Head' V8 coupled to a light truck transmission with 4 forward plus 1 reverse gears

The front bogies are connected together. When the steering wheel is turned, they move side to side to 'warp' the track in the direction opposite to a desired turn

During the Mk II production run, the armoured hull was assembled using more and more welding vs almost all riveted construction used at the start. However, early Mk II (and all Mk I remanufactured to Mk II standards) had the same basic Mk I type hull assembly. Thus, many Universal Carrier Mk IIs have hull construction that is indistinguishable from the Mk I.

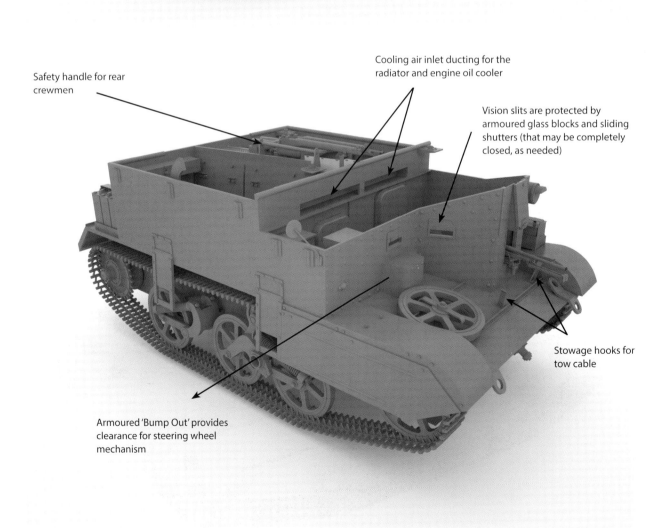

Idler wheel is movable to adjust track tension

Light truck drum brakes

Automotive differential

Continued turning of the steering wheel causes the rear drum brake on the inside of the desired turn to function, slowing down the inside trackwhile power is transferred by the differential to the outside track

Cooling air inlet ducting for the radiator and engine oil cooler

Safety handle for rear crewmen

Vision slits are protected by armoured glass blocks and sliding shutters (that may be completely closed, as needed)

Stowage hooks for tow cable

Armoured 'Bump Out' provides clearance for steering wheel mechanism

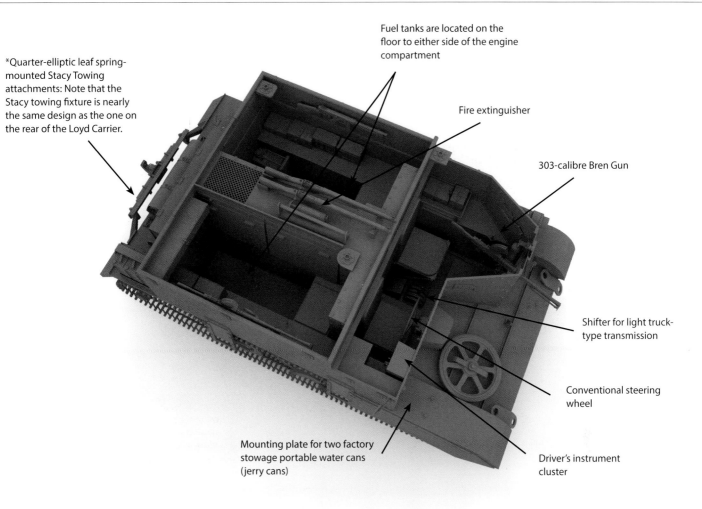

Fuel tanks are located on the floor to either side of the engine compartment

Fire extinguisher

303-calibre Bren Gun

*Quarter-elliptic leaf spring-mounted Stacy Towing attachments: Note that the Stacy towing fixture is nearly the same design as the one on the rear of the Loyd Carrier.

Shifter for light truck-type transmission

Conventional steering wheel

Mounting plate for two factory stowage portable water cans (jerry cans)

Driver's instrument cluster

Diagramatic sketch of a Universal Carrier Mk II ighlighting the Mk ll recognition features:

1.   Deep wading kit mounts
2.   Tubular edge guards
3.   Side steps for crewmen
4.   Single headlight mounting
5.   Tow cable hooks
6.   Spare road wheel
7.   Redesigned fenders
8.   Mount for factory water can stowage

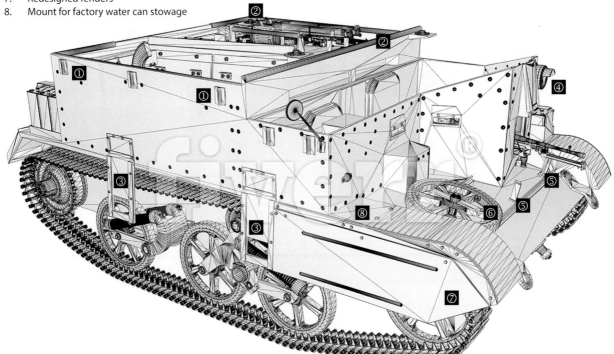

In Service and in Action

The Battle of France

When war broke out in September 1939, it was the Scout Carrier version of the vehicle that was allocated to the seven mechanized divisional cavalry regiments that accompanied the British Expeditionary Force (BEF) to France, 44 carriers being assigned to each regiment alongside 28 light tanks. Ten Bren Carriers were initially assigned to the support companies of each infantry battalion.

In the months following its deployment to France, the BEF, which was placed under French command and took up positions on the left of the French First Army, was mainly occupied in preparing defences along its section of the Franco-Belgian border. When the Germans launched their offensive on the Western Front on 10 May 1940, the Bren Carrier platoons inevitably became involved in the confused fighting that accompanied the BEF's initial action and subsequent fighting retreat to Dunkirk.

When the BEF's columns advanced into Belgium on 12 May the troops experienced mixed impressions, as one eyewitness related:

'The procession on the roads has drawn villagers to their doors. They sit on chairs on the pavement watching the cavalcade go by. British guns (medium and light) draped in dust-sheets, Bren carriers, motor lorries – all the impedimenta of war; and on the other side of the road, speeding towards us, those fleeing from war as from the plague – thousands upon thousands of refugees.'

One incident that occurred during the fighting around Arras saw the posthumous award of the Victoria Cross to the commander of a carrier platoon, Lieutenant the Honourable Christopher Furness. The citation, published in the London Gazette after the war, tells the story:

Top: Men of a territorial battalion of the Highland Light Infantry, City of Glasgow Regiment, on exercise with their Bren Gun Carriers in the UK, 1939. (IWM)

Above: A British Carrier crew lend a hand to a French farmer breaking the soil during the Phoney War period. (ECP Armees)

Left: Troops of the 2nd Monmouthshire Regiment leap from their Universal Carrier during an exercise near Newry, County Down, Northern Ireland. (Wikimedia Commons)

Continues page 49

Machine Gun Carrier No. 2 Mk I
An early Bren Gun Carrier from a batch built by Thorneycroft. Note the folding, sloped plate behind the third crew member's compartment. The vehicle is armed with a 0.303-inch Vickers machine gun. The tools for maintaining the tracks etc are located at the rear of the vehicle.

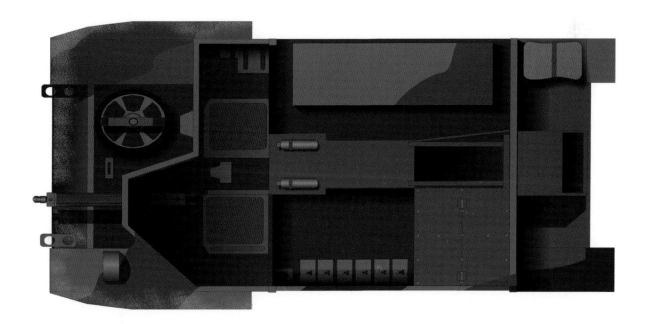

Universal Carrier Mk I
The Universal Carrier Mk I depicting two headlights, he multiple box stowage arrangement at the rear and block-shaped wood or rubber guards. The Caunter camouflage scheme was applied during the Mk I's service.

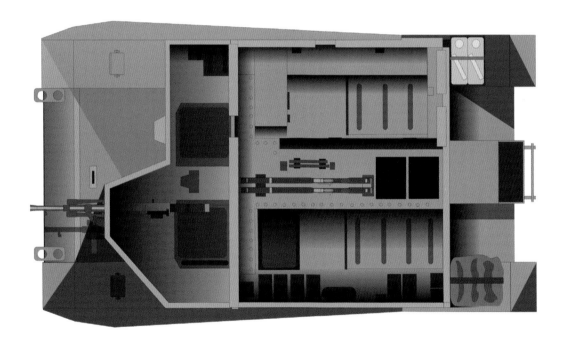

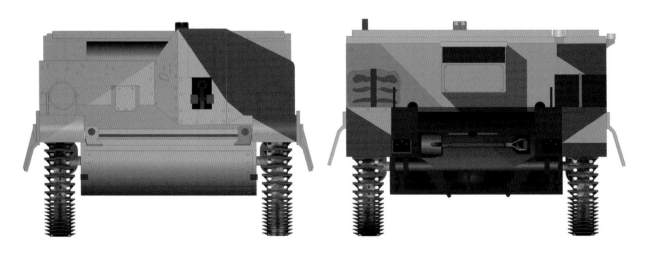

Mortar Carrier
It was originally envisaged that the carrier would be developed to carry out specific
tasks, such as a dedicated mortar carrier, but all these roles were combined in a single
vehicle, the Universal Carrier. About 400 mortar carriers were in fact produced in
Australia, most being delivered to the Chinese Nationalist Army.

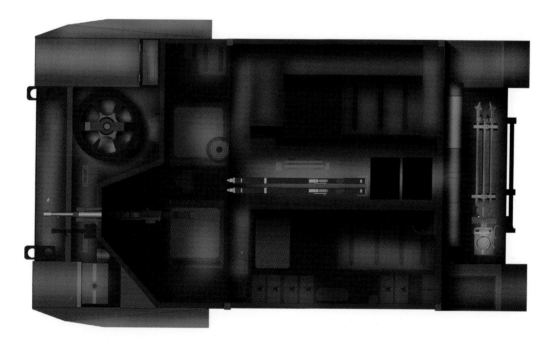

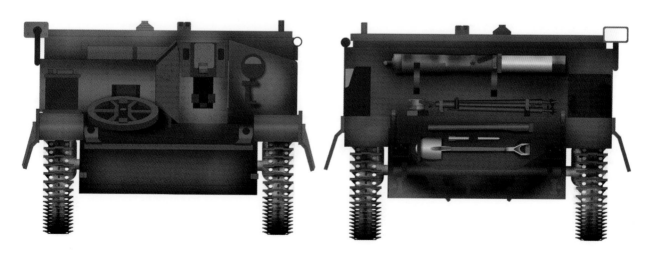

Universal Carrier Mk II
Upgrades that make the Mk II recognizable from the Mk I include the single headlight mounting, the missing fender with the crew step, the POL can stowage and the spare road wheel. Tubular gurads on the top edges of the hull armour have replaced the block-like guards of the Mk I and at the rear, the revised stowage box and towing hook and frame.

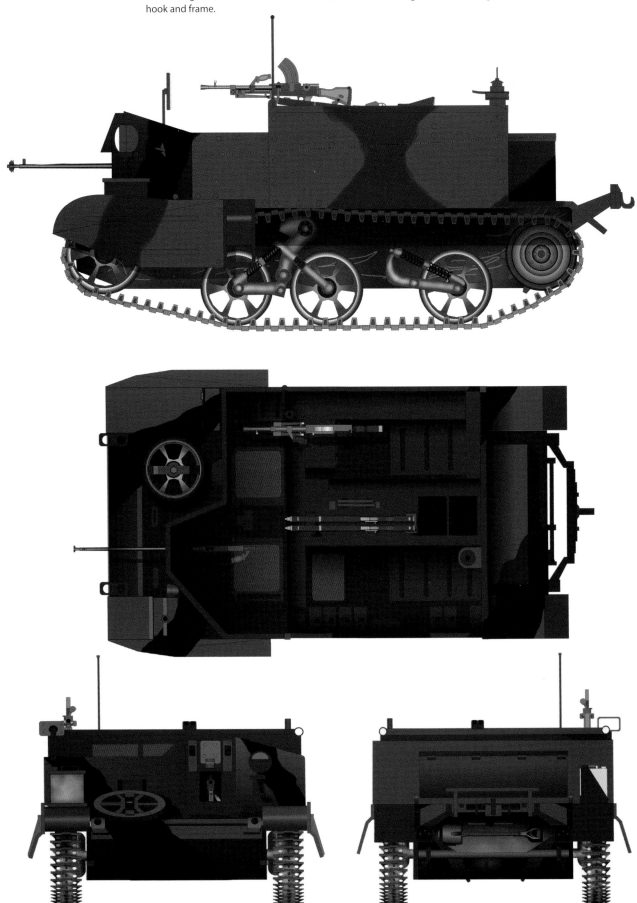

T-16 Carrier

The Carrier, Universal, T-16, Mark I was a significantly improved vehicle based upon those built by Ford of Canada, manufactured under Lend-Lease by Ford in the United States from March 1943 to 1945. It was longer than the Universal Carrier with an extra road wheel on the rear bogie. The engine was a Mercury-division 3.9 litre displacement Ford Flathead.

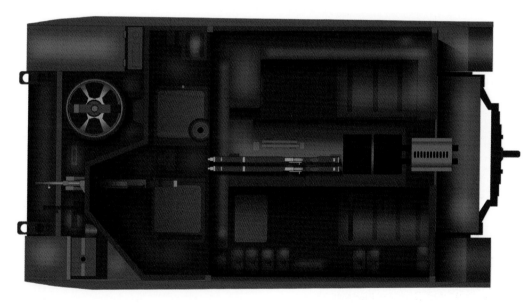

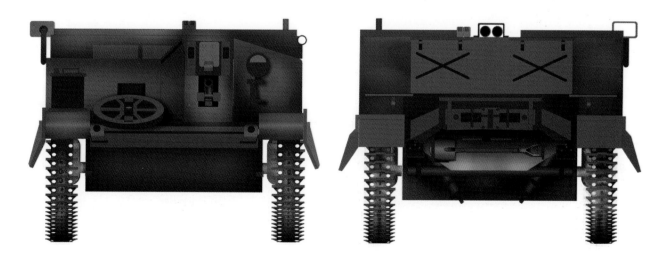

2-Pounder Anti-Tank Gun Carrier

The 2-pdr Anti-tank Gun Carrier (Aust), also known as the carrier, 2-pdr Tank Attack, was a heavily modified and lengthened LP2 Carrier with a fully traversable quick-firing 2-pdr anti-tank gun mounted on a platform at the rear and the engine moved to the front left of the vehicle. Stowage was provided for 112 rounds of 2-pdr ammunition. 200 were produced and used for training.

Wasp Mk IIC
The Wasp was a flamethrower-equipped variant of the Universal Carrier Mks I and II.
The Mk I had a fixed flamethrower on the front of the vehicle fed from two fuel tanks
with a combined capacity of 100 gallons. 1000 were produced. In the Mk II, the flame
projector was situated in the co-driver's position. The vehicle seen here is the Wasp
Mk IIC, a Canadian-built version.

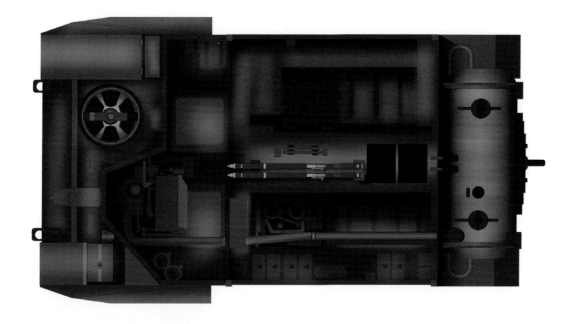

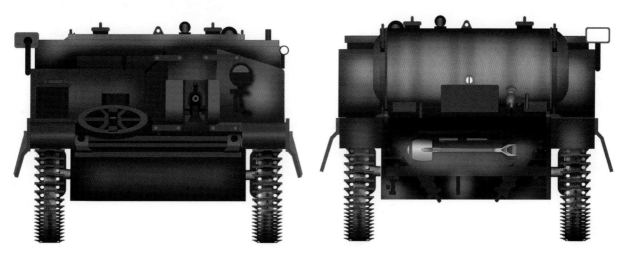

Panzerjäger Bren 731(e)
Some Universal Carriers captured by the Germans were converted to the role of tank
destroyer. Given the designation Panzerjäger Bren 731(e), this example was fitted
with a triple rack for transporting the Panzerschreck man-portable rocket-launched
anti-tank weapon. It was armed with an MG42 machine gun.

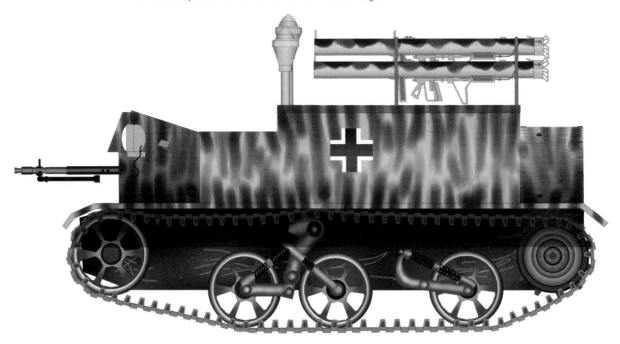

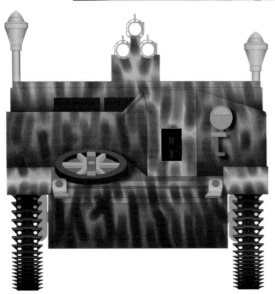

UNIVERSAL CARRIER MK II

Royal Artillery Observation Post

1/72 Scale
Timothy Neate

The IBG 1/72 scale Universal Carrier No 2 Mk II measures 52 x 27mm and is a good base for conversions and detailing. With this in mind I decided to use it to make a Royal Artillery Observation Post (OP) Carrier, which carries all the necessary equipment to observe and correct the fall of artillery fire on the battlefield. It has a crew of four, a driver, wireless operator, OP assistant (lance bombardier) and a captain/ Forward Observation Officer (FOO).

The 43rd Wessex Division marking was sourced on the internet and the Royal Artillery arm of service markings were drawn on a computer. Both were printed onto laser water slide decal paper from Crafty Computer paper.

The figures, all in their positions, looking natural. The captain observing through his binoculars, the OP assistant looking on, the wireless operator receiving a message and the driver ready to move on command.

The one Pound coin highlights how incredibly small this models is.

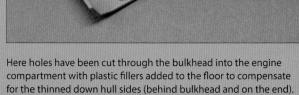

The manpack No. 18 wireless with canvas cover, the No. 11 vehicle wireless and the battery tray scratch built from plastic card before painting and fitting.

Here holes have been cut through the bulkhead into the engine compartment with plastic fillers added to the floor to compensate for the thinned down hull sides (behind bulkhead and on the end).

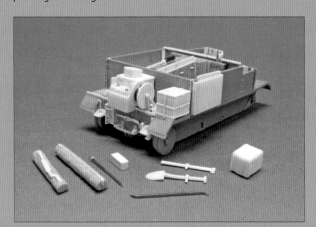

These equipment bags were made from Milliput and the canvas covered charging set was constructed as a plastic card box with creases carved into the surface. The pioneer tools were painted separately before being added to the storage frame on the lower hull.

The crew figures are painted and detailed with Humbrol enamels, with the standing figures measuring only 25mm high.

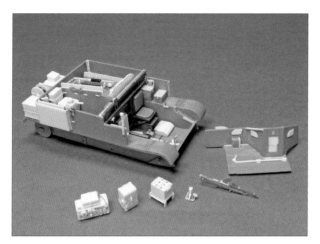

The extra detail added to the forward compartment can be seen here before the front of the hull was fitted. The Bren gun and lifting jack from the kit were modified and the scratch built wireless sets stand ready to be painted.

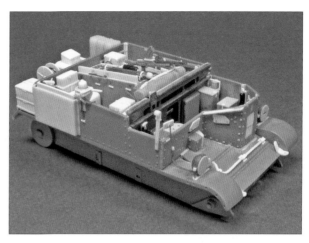

Stowage for the artillery board is on the outside of the hull, with the track adjustment tool mounted across the front of the hull. The details on the lights were improved and new front towing eyes added.

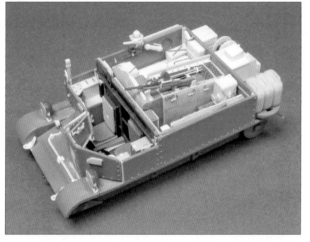

A view of the detail inside the hull showing structural detail as well as the junior compressor which is mounted next to the aerial mount with a cable leading to the wireless set, and the visor mechanisms.

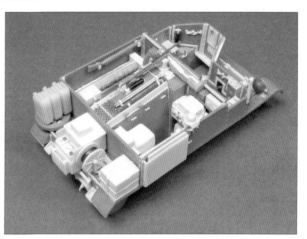

The arrangement of equipment and stowage on the rear is visible here, along with a rifle stowed on the inside of the hull.

Right: The officer and OP assistant placed in their positions to making sure they have good contact with their surroundings and looking natural. Dried mud has been added to the lower hull with a mixture of plaster of Paris and enamel paint ready for the running gear to be added later.

The engine cover was painted and finished, but kept loose to allow easier access for adding components in the carrier's confined space. The No. 11 wireless set has had all its dials and details painted and is positioned on the right against the bulkhead above the battery tray.

The rear of the carrier is crammed with equipment and topped off with a large canvas roll sculpted from Milliput. The neatly rolled putty was applied to the model to take on the contours of the equipment beneath. Once the Milliput had hardened it can be popped off and carved into a canvas roll.

The weathering on the running gear is a wash of 90% white spirit/10% Humbrol No. 72 enamel paint. The dried mud was sparingly stippled on using a mix of plaster of Paris and Humbrol No. 26 and No. 72 in separate mixes. Finally, a black-brown pin wash was applied to areas to suggest oil/grease seepage.

The wireless operator is sitting in a crouched position in front of the No. 11 wireless set with his helmet ready behind him. The manpack No. 18 wireless set is stowed at the rear on the OP assistant's side of the carrier.

LOYD CARRIER
Anti-Tank Platoon, 1st Battalion, The Rifle Brigade, 22nd Armoured Regiment
1/35 Scale
Michael Roof

Arguably the most photographed Loyd Carriers are the ones pictured by German PK photographers after the Battle of Villers-Bocage. When Bronco released its Loyd Carrier kit (CB35188), I knew my subject would have to be one of these Villers-Bocage carriers. However, I wanted to show my carrier as it might have looked in the minutes before Michael Wittmann began his renowned attack down Route National 175 against the parked 7th Armoured Division column in June, 1944. The Loyd Carriers belonged to the Anti-Tank Platoon of the 1st Battalion, The Rifle Brigade of the 22nd Armored Regiment. I coupled the Bronco kit with Riich's OQF 6-pdr Anti-Tank Gun (RV35018) as the basis of my scene. Neither the Bronco Loyd Carrier kit nor the Riich 6-pdr kit is for the fainthearted modeller. They are both extremely well detailed, and include PE parts. However, that detail comes at the cost of numerous small parts, close fit tolerances and delicate sub-assemblies. Having said that, the kits are certainly 'buildable' and will reward the modeller with beautiful replicas of the prototypes.

Bronco gives the modeller several options with the Loyd Carrier, and I referred to the many photos of the Villers-Bocage carriers. I selected the spoked wheels, and I left the fastener heads on the hull sides since both features matched the photos. I folded up the front bow of the tilt frame and added a rolled up tarp/tilt made from two part epoxy putty with lead foil straps and PE buckles.

The subject Loyd Carriers also had large rolls of concertina wire carried atop the tilt frame. I replicated this feature with barbed wire from RMG Resin Models (RM013). I also added a set of gun cleaning rods made from brass tube along with British WD copies of Jerry cans and 'flimsy' cans, also from Bronco.

The carrier and anti-tank gun were painted with various Tamiya paints and with artist oil paint washes and highlights. The markings are a mixture of waterslide decals left over from other projects and Woodland Scenics dry transfers. The registration numbers were matched to the reference photos.

The crew figures are all modified Bronco figures with resin Hornet heads and hands. They were all primed with airbrushed Tamiya flat white. Over the primer, I undercoated the figures by hand brushing various hobby acrylics, mostly from Vallejo. Once the acrylic undercoating was dry, the figures were fully painted with artist oils. All of the insignia were hand painted.

BREN GUN CARRIER
German Army, Benghazi, North Africa, 1941
1/35 Scale
Morgen Violet-Harris

This is Riich Models 2.8cm s.PZ.B.41 auf Selbsfahrlatte Bren Carrier 731 (e), based on a photo taken of a vehicle captured and pressed into service be the German army in Benghazi, Libya 1941. The model is comprised of what was originally two separate kits with over 450 fine- and well-detailed parts used in a subject a third the size of modern armour models. The first part uses a modification of Riich Models earlier Universal Carriers which includes nine plastic sprues, one clear sprue, 32 small springs, a length of chain and a length of string. Bronco's 2.8cm sPzB.41 anti-tank rifle using three grey sprues makes the second part, two photo-etch sheets and a small decal sheet are shared between both Riich and Bronco parts.

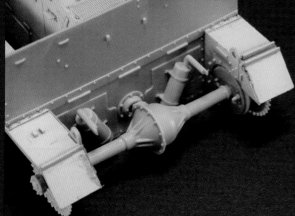

In this instance the kit instructions are incorrect, following them will cause a misalignment of the transmission causing it not to seat correctly (a copy of the corrected ones are included from the Riich models website). I found this out after it was too late to fix.

The instructions don't show the Pb19. It actually has a side part that needs to be bent downwards and attached to the side of the kit fender.

Detail on the kit parts is very fine with small attachment points allowing for the easy detachment of parts. The builder has two ways to approach building this model, the first, following the instructions, which would entail either a lot of stop-start building and painting or painting after most of the building, but finding it difficult to paint some areas. The second option and the one I chose is to study the instructions well and assemble most of the internals of the vehicle before adding the vehicle sides and working on the external areas. This minimizes the painting sessions required for the vehicle interior. Whichever way the builder chooses to go I would suggest obtaining as much reference material as possible and referencing the top down view on the marking sheet due to many sections of the instruction steps being unclear in terms of the correct placement of parts.

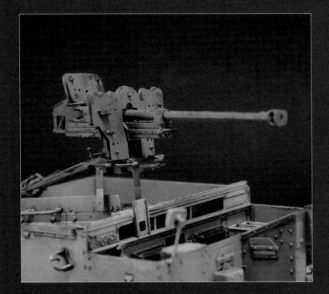

The 2.8cm sPzB.41 anti-tank rifle goes together quite easily, the only quandary being the instructions depict hand-holds on parts of the guns armour but none are supplied either in plastic or photo-etch. The gun was probably grey before arriving in North Africa where it would have been repainted desert yellow. To simulate that I base coated Tamiya XF-63 German Grey, applied a coat of hair spray then sprayed Tamiya XF-60. Then, using water and stiff brushes I gave the XF-60 a well-chipped appearance to help give contrast to this dusty, but relatively unchipped, Bren Gun Carrier.

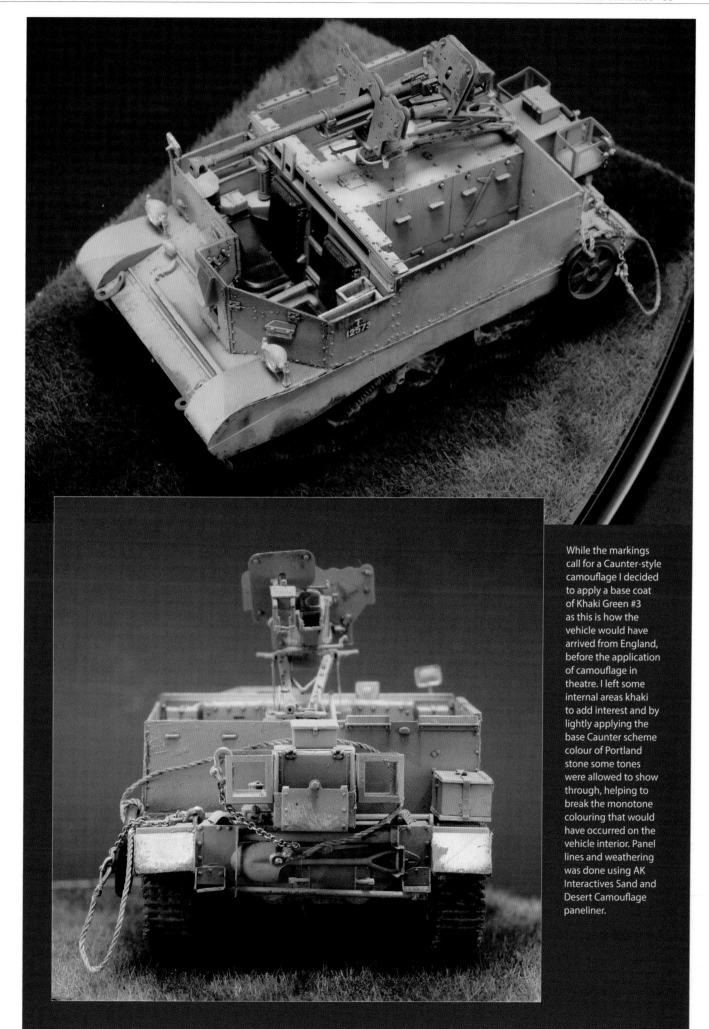

While the markings call for a Caunter-style camouflage I decided to apply a base coat of Khaki Green #3 as this is how the vehicle would have arrived from England, before the application of camouflage in theatre. I left some internal areas khaki to add interest and by lightly applying the base Caunter scheme colour of Portland stone some tones were allowed to show through, helping to break the monotone colouring that would have occurred on the vehicle interior. Panel lines and weathering was done using AK Interactives Sand and Desert Camouflage paneliner.

The original photo showed a spare wheel mounted on the vehicle's side. This was not included in the kit parts, so I made a mould of one of the kit wheels and cast a spare.

Detail of the interior of the vehicle.

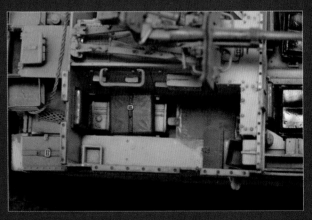

Exterior painting was applied in much the same way as the vehicle interior, adding the rest of the colour used in Caunter camouflage before sealing and weathering. This particular vehicle served in North Africa and the photo of it shows the top half covered in dust, it also shows the vehicle parked in a muddy field with its tracks and wheels covered in mud, a nice contrast that I wanted to replicate. I sprayed heavily thinned Tamiya Buff and Desert Yellow colours in multiple coats to achieve the dust effect. Ammo of Mig Mud splashes mixed with various tones of mud coloured pigment was applied across the running gear and bottom of the vehicle. I placed the model on the base while the mud paint was quite wet, these were enamel based paints and seem to have softened and stretched the tracks, causing them buckle.

T-16 CARRIER
Liberation of the Netherlands, 1945
1/35 Scale
Patrick Bernier

This is the Resicast multi-media kit of the T16 Carrier (ref. 35.199). As with any Resicast kits, the casting is top notch and no problem whatsoever was encountered during construction. This carrier, very similar to the more common Universal Carrier, was manufactured in America by Ford.

The most significant difference is the number of wheels, as it has two complete bogie assemblies on each side. It allowed this carrier to be more stable with heavy loads. Therefore, most of them were used as gun tractors.

The rear of the T16 also depicts important changes from the Universal Carrier. Thus, the exhaust system was placed on the top of the motor, just in the middle of both loading sections. The kit's tracks are full resin casting. They come in a few sections but are true to scale and can easily be curbed and put in place with super glue.

This kit will be put in a LVT-4 in a future diorama depicting the Liberation of the Netherlands by Canadian troops. According to official sources, it was impossible to fit one in a LVT. However, a few pictures proved that it was possible. During transport in flooded area, troops had to over-charge their vehicles. No free space was wasted.

Gears from numerous suppliers were added to give some life to the carrier. I added a folded bike from Diopark; a truly tricky build, but a real eye-catcher among the more common gear like helmets and guns. I also added a little teddy bear from Plus Models on the front as the crew's mascot.

The kit was painted in sub-assembly to ease the manipulation and allow for easier painting of details. The base colour was Tamiya Olive Green XF-62 lighted with Tamiya Yellow Green XF-3. The tracks were already fixed before starting the paint job. All the lower parts of the body received intense weathering. The accessories, such as the gear in the carrier were also treated with acrylic paints. After a quick layer of thinned Tamiya Buff XF-57, an overall wash of raw umber (oil paints) was applied on the whole model. After this step I added numerous dots of white, ochre, black and burnt umber on every side of the carrier. All the dots were then blended together with a up-and-down motion using a large brush soaked in taltine (turpentine). Pigments were disseminated everywhere in the inside. The last step consisted of applying a coat of matte varnish from Pebeo.

ACCURATE ARMOUR

The Loyd Carrier Starting and Charging is a 1/35th scale resin model kit. The starting of tank engines from cold, and the need to maintain a wireless watch was a great strain on tank batteries. This version of the Loyd was equipped with batteries, charging unit, slave and test and repair equipment. The Loyd Carrier Personnel depicts the infantry carrier version, equipped to transport eight infantrymen. The third 1/35 resin kit from Accurate Armour is a Loyd Carrier towing a 6-pounder anti-tank gun equipped to transport the gun crew, some 6-pounder rounds and gun spares including a spare wheel (to match the Tamiya or Resicast

6-pounder anti-tank guns). We recommend the Resicast 6 Pr. Anti-tank gun as the best partner for this kit. As a general rule each 6-pounder gun had two carriers, one towing the gun and a second carrier for further ammunition. Sometimes the second carrier would tow a 10-cwt GS trailer (kit K143) with more ammunition and stores. Accurate Armour kits include extensive engine and internal detail, an etched brass detail fret, stowage and a general decal set. The Starting and Charging Carrier also has battery and equipment boxes and the 6-pounder includes extension 6-pounder shields.
Images courtesy of Accurate Armour

Loyd Carrier Starting & Charging #K137   Loyd Carrier Starting & Charging #K137   Loyd Carrier Personnel #K136

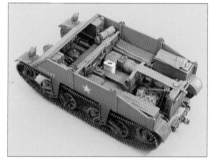  

Loyd Carrier Personnel #K136   Loyd Carrier Towing #K139   Loyd Carrier Towing #K139

AIRFIX

Airfix Vintage Classics presents a 1/76 Bren Gun Carrier & 6-pounder anti-tank gun with 40 green parts and decals for the 51st Highlanders, who landed at Normandy, and includes four crew figures, who fit into the carrier better without their lower halves but are in fact designed for two to man the anti-tank gun and two for the carrier. These guns had crews of six and the two figures for the carrier aren't ideal as one is standing upright, arms at his sides and the other, torso and

head only, should be the driver but has no hands. The figures also sport equipment and uniform inaccuracies and quite a bit of flash. Having said that, the running gear is a one piece moulding of wheels, tracks and suspension and the detail is good for the size. The 6-pounder is small but builds up well with moveable parts, which allow for towing or firing positioning.
Review kit courtesy of HobbyCo
Completed model built by Neil McConnachie

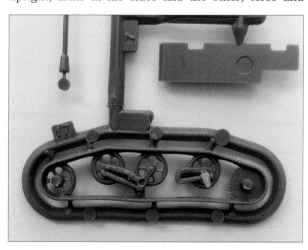 

BRONCO

Bronco's Loyd Carrier No. 2 Mk 2 tracked towing a 6-pounder anti-tank gun tractor. This is a new tool, released in 2015, and offers seven decal options. This build contains a large amount of Photo Etch (PE) and for that reason modellers may find it easier to build it with the bad weather tarp down as by the time you get to that stage you may well be PEed out. There are nice accessory inclusions but as with other things in this kit things don't appear to have been thought through: canteens but no mounting options. The kit has accuracy and fitting issues and is probably best left to veterans and those with a knack for the assembly of very small parts.

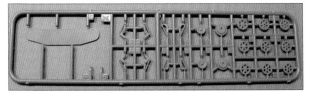

IBG MODELS

IBG have four plastic carrier kits available in 1/72 scale: the Universal Carrier I Mk 1, the Universal Carrier II Mk 2, the Mortar Carrier and the Universal Carrier Mk 1 with Boys 14.5mm. The common sprues are A (chassis, tracks and most other vehicle parts) and X (running gear and track assembly template). The Mk 1 has a bonus sprue that includes boys – not crew mind, no crew members are included in their kits, which is probably just as well since there's no space to insert them – rifles and headlights. The Mk 2 includes a rear winch. The Mortar carrier also has a winch and of course the mortar and ammunition and the Boys and anti-tank rifle kit includes that same bonus sprue supplied with the Mk 1. The fenders are provided on separate sprues for all four kits. There is some flash between the wheel spokes and modellers should take care during assembly not to build the wheel spring facing the same way: one should face the front idler wheel and the other the rear drive sprocket. The track pieces are numerous and very, very small. One modeller suggests it is easier to build the tracks classically, which is not how IBG suggest, building the model to the point where

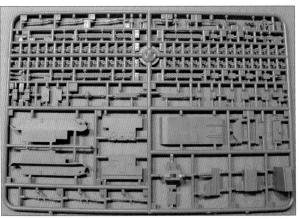

Common sprues A and X.

the running gear can be added and then adding them directly to the kit. Start putting on the tracks moving from the right-most wheel to the left, it's easier to join the track ends together when they wrap around to meet at this point. This is a very laborious, time-consuming part of the build. These are detailed kits with minimal flash and quality fit, instructions and decals and the price isn't bad either. There are plenty of weapons for the spares box too. The side walls, fenders and front hooks, are much too thick and will require sanding

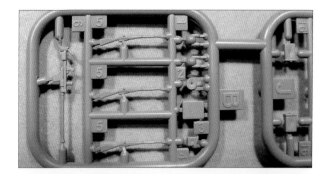

if you want to maintain a less chunky look. A second Bren gun mount would be a nice inclusion too. *Images courtesy of Eduard Ferrer Belda*

Top: Fine detail on the Boys AT rifle.
Above: Detail on Sprue A showing two Bren Guns for spare parts.

Be careful not to fall in the trap of building the wheel springs both facing the same way.

This picture shows the upcoming enhancements. The radio antenna base is fine but side walls require heavy thinning.

Opt for classic track assembly, start putting on the tracks moving from the right most wheel to the left. It's always easier to join the track ends together when they wrap around to meet at this point.

Notice the drive sprocket, awaiting the next track piece.

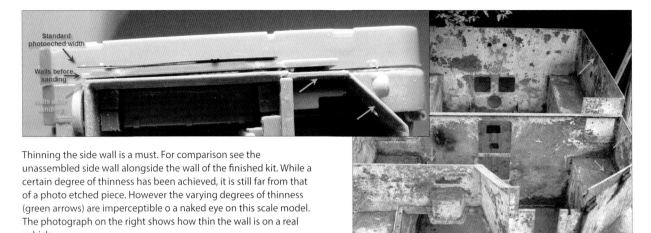

Thinning the side wall is a must. For comparison see the unassembled side wall alongside the wall of the finished kit. While a certain degree of thinness has been achieved, it is still far from that of a photo etched piece. However the varying degrees of thinness (green arrows) are imperceptible o a naked eye on this scale model. The photograph on the right shows how thin the wall is on a real vehicle.

The completed Mk I.

INTERNATIONAL MODELS ASIA

International Models Asia, a small kit manufacturer based in Hong Kong, have the two Australian versions of the carrier available to modellers, the LP3 Mortar Carrier and LP2 Carrier. Both are full resin kits in 1/35 scale.

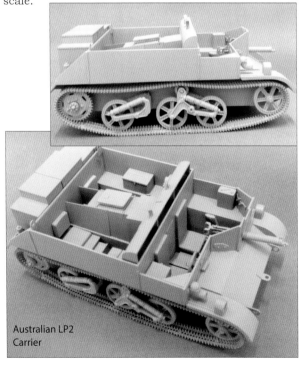

Australian LP2 Carrier

MILICAST

1/76 resin kit maker Milicast has an impressive carrier range: Bren No 1 Mk 1 Carrier; Scout Carrier Mk 1; Conger Mk 1 Mine Clearing Device; Universal Carrier Mk 1 (Scout) (Middle East); Universal Carrier Mk 1 (Scout) (BEF); Universal Carrier Mk 2 (Infantry Carrier); Universal Carrier Mk 3; Gutted Carrier Mk 1 Facine Carrier; Universal carrier No 1 Mk 2 (WT) with 6-pounder anti-tank gun; Universal Carrier Mk 2 (Late) 3-inch mortar-firing position; Universal Carrier Mk 2 (Late) 3-inch mortar-stowed position; Universal carrier Mk 1 (Rivetted) 3-inch mortar-firing position; Universal Carrier Mk 1 (Rivetted) 3-inch mortar-stowed position; Universal carrier No 1 Mk 2 (WT) with deep wading equipment; Universal Carrier No 1 Mk 2 (WT) (Late) with deep wading equipment; Loyd Carrier (Middle East Pattern); Loyd Mk 1 Personnel Carrier; Australian Carrier LP1; Carrier Machine Gun No 2 Mk 1; Cavalry Carrier Mk 1; Wasp Mk 2C, Carrier Mk 1; Carrier Mk 1 Wasp Mk 2 Flamethrower; Carrier Mk 1 Wasp Mk 2C (Canadian); Loyd Battery Charger Carrier; British Carrier Infantry, designed and produced by Dan Taylor Modelworks; Dragon Mk 3 (BEF). 20mm scale water slide decals from Aleran Decals can be purchased solely from Milicast and obviously they recommend those for their kits.

Images and models courtesy of Milicast Models

#BB025 Universal Carrier No.1 Mk II (WT) with Deep Wading equipment.

#BB217 Universal Carrier Mk II (Infantry Carrier).

#UK196 Carrier Mk I Wasp Mk II Flamethrower.

PLASTIC SOLDIER

In 1/72 scale the Plastic Soldier Company has two carrier products: an Easy Assembly British Universal Carrier 1/72 scale with three models and 12 crew figures with options to build either a Mk 1 or a Mk 2 and a Reinforcement British Universal carrier. Both sold out at the time of writing but can be picked up second hand or where stock is still available through distributors. They also have a 15mm Universal Carrier with miniatures and six models included, each sprue includes the options to build a 2-inch mortar, 3-inch mortar, Vickers .50-calibre, AOP and two Wasp flamethrowers. Also in 15mm is the Reinforcements Universal carrier kit.

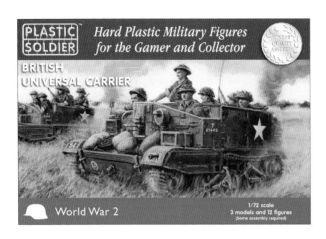

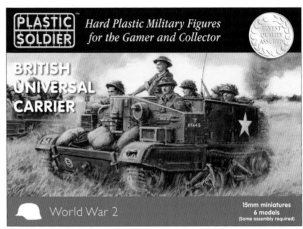

RESICAST

Resicast have four full kits available for carriers, the T-16 #351199 T-16; the Bren Carrier #351203 Bren Carrier; the Scout Carrier #351205 Scout Carrier; the Windsor Carrier #351212. The T-16 instructions are the new-style, photo-lead type and the 200-odd parts are detailed to a high standard. The kit give road wheel options, the later version disc- or more common spoke-style wheels. This is true also of the bulk head and the instructions assist with selection depending on what version you're building. The tracks are flexible and fairly easy to work with and the fenders are in PE form. The Bren Carrier is the highly detailed kit modellers now expect from Resicast, and includes stowage items like grenade boxes, track adjuster levers, spare parts box, stowage bins and weapons. The Scout Carrier is highly praised as being cast with model makers in mind. The last couple of pages in the instruction booklet contains reference photographs too.

Other Resicast products for carriers include:
352285 Carrier tracks (for Tamiya Universal Carrier)
352293 Stowage set (for Tamiya Universal Carrier)
352299 Deep wading kit (for Tamiya Universal Carrier)
352335 Stowage set (for 4.2-inch mortar Windsor Carrier)
352336 Stowage set (for 6-pounder Windsor Carrier)
352353 Stowage set (for Riich Carrier Mk 1)
All other Resicast carrier kits and conversion kits are currently out of production, but demand is high and they may well come back into production.
Images courtesy of Resicast Models

35.1205
Scout Carrier

Complete resin kit
Scale 1/35

Includes resin, and
photoetched parts

Master by
George Moore

Model assembled and
painted by C. Nachtergael

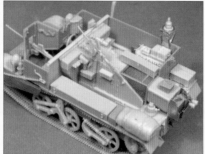

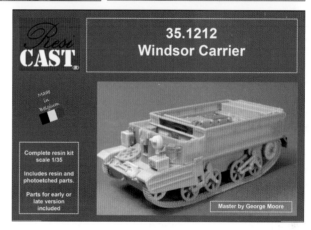

35.1203
Bren Carrier

Complete resin kit
Scale 1/35

Includes resin, and
photoetched parts

Master by
George Moore

35.1212
Windsor Carrier

Complete resin kit
scale 1/35

Includes resin and
photoetched parts.

Parts for early or
late version
included

Master by George Moore

RIICH.MODELS

Riich Model's 1/35 scale range in carriers is a welcome plastic kit for this iconic military vehicle. The Universal Carrier Mk 1 (with crew) offers a few options: a choice of British or Canadian pattern head lights, alternate fender layout with either the small front fender guards or just with the full length bolt strip along the outer fenders as well as alternate storage arrangements. The assembly is complicated but the fit very good. The figures are adequate, the uniform detail is good, the facial features not so good and fitting them into the hull is no small task. Riich Models also has a Mk 1 with 3-inch mortar available. Two Mk 2s are offered by Ricch Models, a Universal Carrier MMG Mk 2 (.303 Vickers MMG Carrier) and a Universal Carrier Mk 2 with full interior. The Mk 2 build-up is described by modeller Michael Scharf thus: "This is a challenging build for experienced modellers. Having a complete interior, you must study the directions and plan carefully to make painting stress-free. Many of the photo-etched-metal pieces have complicated bends not shown clearly in the directions. Consequently, it took a whopping 52 hours to build a model not much bigger than a jeep. Still, it all results in a stunning model". The Mk 2 comes with a crew variation: British Commonwealth in winter uniform 1943–1945 and a limited edition British Airborne Universal Carrier Mk 3 & Welbike Mk 2 is also available to modellers. September saw the release of a new carrier, the WASP Mk 2.

Images courtesy of Riich.Models

Universal Carrier Mk II.

TAMIYA

Tamiya's first British Universal Carrier Mk 2 gave the modeller a choice of seven colour schemes and markings. In North Africa (1st Armoured Division and 21st Indian Division) they were painted dark yellow and in Europe and Burma, dark green (3rd and 50th Infantry divisions, 7th Armoured Division, the 27th Brigade and in Burma, the 7th Brigade). The 1994 European Campaign release added a Royal Canadian Army decal option for the 3rd Infantry Division and replaced the 7th Armoured and 27th and 7th brigades for the 1st Armoured and 78th Infantry divisions. The Forced Reconnaissance release in 2001 has more specific decal options, three are Northwest Europe (Guards Armoured Division, 1st Battalion, Grenadier Guards; 7th Armoured Division, 131st Infantry Brigade, 5th Queens Royal Regiment, 1st Battalion; 3rd Infantry Division, 185th Infantry Brigade, 2nd Battalion. Kings Shropshire Light Infantry) and one Tunisia (6th Armoured Division, The Rifle Brigade, 10th Battalion). The original tooling is now over 40 years old, so the moulding is bulky by today's standards but with patience these can be filed down to make them appear thinner and the addition of spares and stowage can hide areas where the detail is poor. To assist with painting the small, yet very visible interior, modellers might consider three sub-assemblies: the main hull, running gear, crew and driver compartments; frontal armour and glacis plates to allow access to the driver compartment; engine housing onto which the Vickers heavy machine gun would be mounted along with stowage. Tamiya also has a 1/48 Universal Carrier with four decal options. Overall the 1/48 kit is a decent model with fairly simple breakdown, good fit and details on the parts like as those on the weapons but as with the 1/35 kit the tracks are inadequate, for this kit they are toy-like and let down the final appearance.

Images courtesy www.scalemodellingnow.com

Rubicon Models will be releasing a Loyd Carrier Mk II resin kit in 1/56 scale in 2019.

'Lieutenant the Honourable C. Furness was in command of the Carrier Platoon, Welsh Guards, during the period 17th-24th May, 1940, when his Battalion formed part of the garrison of Arras. During this time his Platoon was constantly patrolling in advance of or between the widely dispersed parts of the perimeter, and fought many local actions with the enemy. Lieutenant Furness displayed the highest qualities of leadership and dash on all these occasions and imbued his command with a magnificent offensive spirit.

'During the evening of 23rd May, Lieutenant Furness was wounded when on patrol but he refused to be evacuated. By this time the enemy, considerably reinforced, had encircled the town on three sides and withdrawal to Douai was ordered during the night of 23rd-24th May. Lieutenant Furness's Platoon, together with a small force of light tanks, were ordered to cover the withdrawal of the transport consisting of over 40 vehicles. About 0230 hours, 24th May, the enemy attacked on both sides of the town. At one point the enemy advanced to the road along which the transport columns were withdrawing, bringing them under very heavy small arms and anti-tank gun fire. Thus the whole column was blocked and placed in serious jeopardy. Immediately Lieutenant Furness, appreciating the seriousness of the situation, and in spite of his wounds, decided to attack the enemy, who were located in a strongly entrenched position behind wire. Lieutenant Furness advanced with three Carriers, supported by the light tanks. At once the enemy opened up with very heavy fire from small arms and anti-tank guns. The light tanks were put out of action, but Lieutenant Furness continued to advance. He reached the enemy position and circled it several times at close range, inflicting heavy losses. All three Carriers were hit and most of their crews killed or wounded. His own Carrier was disabled and the driver and Bren gunner killed. He then engaged the enemy in personal hand-to-hand combat until he was killed. His magnificent act of self sacrifice against hopeless odds, and when already wounded, made the enemy withdraw for the time being and enabled the large column of vehicles to get clear unmolested and covered the evacuation of some of the wounded of his own Carrier Platoon and the light tanks.'

During the BEF's fighting withdrawal to the Channel coast the surviving Bren Carriers, mostly operating with rearguard formations, fought many actions with advancing enemy reconnaissance patrols, and proved invaluable in maintaining contact with BEF units. It was a far from easy task, as one British officer recorded:

'The roads were congested with MT and blocked in places with abandoned transport: there were few maps and these only 1/250,000: the route had not been reconnoitred: the MT drivers were tired out.

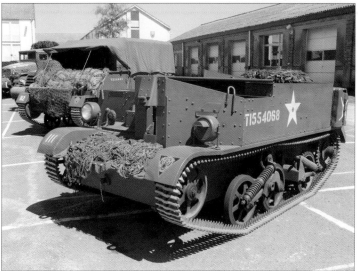

So it was not surprising that part of the convoy went astray. Captain Mansell and I and the three carriers got lost too.'

Another eyewitness mentions the chaotic scenes that accompanied the retreat:

'Every road scoring the landscape was one thick mass of transport and troops, great long lines of them stretching far back to the eastern horizon, and all the lines converging towards the one focus – Dunkirk. Ambulances, lorries, trucks, Bren-gun carriers, artillery columns – everything except tanks – all crawling along those roads in well-defined lines over the flat, featureless country in the late afternoon sunshine, provided an impressive and memorable picture of two modern armies in retreat. Under their greyish camouflage paint they resembled from a distance slow-moving rivers of muddy-coloured lava from some far-off eruption.'

Bren Gun Carriers also took part in the operations conducted by the 51st Highland Division at St Valery-en-Caux during the first days of June 1940, a gallant last stand that resulted in most of the division being captured.

Top: Bren Gun Carriers passing Belgian refugees and dispirited Belgian soldiers on the Brussels-Louvain road, 12 May 1940. (IWM)

Above: This carrier bears the insignia of the Belgian I Corps, which defended Liege before being forced to retreat by superior German forces. (Belgian Army Museum)

Scout Carriers moving through Louvain, Belgium, on 14 May 1940. (IWM)

German soldiers passing abandoned Bren Gun Carriers as they approach Dunkirk pulling a 37mm anti-tank gun, early June 1940. (Bundesarchiv)

Abandoned Scout Carrier on the road to Dunkirk, May 1940. (Wikimedia Commons)

Of necessity, the BEF's surviving Bren Carriers were abandoned on the approach to Dunkirk, to fall into German hands. Some of the more serviceable examples were converted to the following roles and received German designations: 2cm Flak 38 auf Fahrgestell Bren(e): Single barrel German 2cm Flak 38 cannon mounted over the engine compartment of a captured Bren Carrier.

3.7cm Pak auf Fahrgestell Bren(e): Captured carrier of 1940, fitted with a 3.7 cm PaK (Panzerabwehrkanone) anti-tank gun.

Panzerjäger Bren 731(e): Bren carriers captured by the Germans and fitted with a triple rack for transporting the Panzerschreck man-portable anti-tank weapon.

Bren Carriers were also deployed to Norway in support of the Anglo-French expeditionary force in April-June 1940, although many were lost when the cargo vessel on which they were loaded, the MV Cedarbank, was torpedoed and sunk on 21 April by the German submarine U26 en route to Andalsnes.

After the Battle of France, a new formation entitled the Reconnaissance Corps was established to provide the mobile spearhead of the British Army's infantry divisions. Reconnaissance regiments were organised into a headquarters squadron (including anti-tank, signals and mortar troops) and three reconnaissance (or recce) squadrons. The scale of equipment for each regiment was 63 Carriers and 28 Humber Scout Cars. Each recce squadron comprised three scout troops and an assault troop. Infantry rifle battalions were originally issued with 10 Universal Carriers for carrying support weapons and other equipment, this figure increasing to 21 in 1941 and 33 by 1943.

Greece and Crete

Following the Italian invasion of Greece in October 1940, 77 Universal Carriers supplied by Britain were employed by the Hellenic Army's 19th Mechanized Division. When German forces invaded Greece in April 1941, mixed Universal Carrier and motorcycle reconnaissance detachments preceded the deployment of Hellenic Army regiments to their designated battle areas, suffering serious losses to German armour and air attack before the remnants of the 19th Division were forced to surrender. Universal Carriers were also used by British, Australian and New Zealand forces in Greece, the survivors being withdrawn to Crete, which was overwhelmed in turn in May 1941.

North Africa, Sicily and Italy

When Germany's Axis partner Italy entered the war in June 1940, the British forces in Egypt suddenly found themselves under serious threat. Although formations such as the British 7th Armoured Division did have the use of Carriers in the successful

campaign against Italian forces, there were never enough, and those that were available were often in poor condition. Among the British and Empire formations that took part in the campaign was the Australian 6th Division Cavalry Regiment, which had been in the Middle East since January 1940 and had trained on Universal Carriers in Palestine. At the end of 1940 the regiment moved into the Western Desert, where it joined British forces in readiness for the coming offensive, launched on 9 December. Two days later the regiment became the first unit of the 2nd Australian Imperial Force (AIF) to go into action when one of its squadrons fought a sharp engagement against the Italians holding Garn el Grein and Fort Maddalena on 11 and 12 December. By 21 December British forces had captured Sidi Barrani and the desert was now open for the 6th Division's advance along the Libyan coast.

On 3 January 1941 the division attacked and captured the Italian fortress of Bardia. The regiment's A Squadron, under the command of Major Denzil Macarthur-Onslow, who went on to command the 4th Armoured Brigade, supported the attack with its twenty serviceable Carriers, their firepower increased by the addition of Vickers 0.303-inch machine guns. Tobruk was the next Italian fort to be captured, with the regiment again in support and covering the 19th Brigade's advance. The regiment, though, was under-equipped and without its full compliment of vehicles, using only machine gun carriers. To compensate for this, A Squadron was partly re-equipped with captured Italian light tanks, which had large kangaroos painted on the hulls and turrets to distinguish them from enemy vehicles. After Tobruk, the regiment

was used as part of the advance guard in the capture of Derna and then Benghazi.

In April the unit moved to Helwan, where it was equipped with Vickers light tanks and machine gun carriers, and operated with British troops in capturing Sollum. Towards the end of May the regiment moved to Palestine, where it came under the command of the 7th Division for the imminent invasion of Syria. The regiment experienced its heaviest fighting during the Syrian campaign, which began on 7 June. A Squadron was attached to the 21st Brigade and advanced along the coast, where the rugged hills made it difficult to manoeuvre the tanks and carriers. The squadron was relieved by one of the 9th Division Cavalry Regiment's squadrons on 13 and 14 June. C Squadron, meanwhile, was with the 25th Brigade, and advanced along the Rosh Pinna road, engaging strong enemy defences at Fort Khirbe. C Squadron was

Australian soldiers in a Mk I Bren Gun Carrier, identified by its sloping rear, on exercise in Egypt.
(Australian War Memorial)

New Zealand troops and a Bren Carrier in Egypt, 1941. (Via John McKenna)

Bren Carriers advancing en masse though the Western Desert, 1941.
(Via John McKenna)

relieved by B Squadron, which was later attacked by Vichy French tanks that were supported by heavy artillery and machine-gun fire, which forced the Australians to withdraw. The regiment remained in Syria as part of the occupation force and returned to Australia in March 1942.

Meanwhile, the 2nd New Zealand Division, which had sustained heavy losses in the Battle of Crete before being evacuated to Egypt, had been integrated into the order of battle of the British Eighth Army, and participated in the desert battles of 1942. The biggest of these was the Battle of Gazala, fought in May and June 1942, when General Erwin Rommel's Afrika Korps succeeded in outflanking the allied defensive line and forced the British Eighth Army into retreat. As the British fell back towards the Egyptian frontier, the coastal fortress of Tobruk, which had withstood an eight-month siege during Rommel's first offensive in 1941 before being relieved, now found itself isolated and under siege again.

This time, Rommel's tanks were successful and the Tobruk defences were quickly overwhelmed. Among the defending forces were the 2/7th Gurkhas, fighting alongside the 2nd Queen's Own Cameron Highlanders and the Indian troops of the 2/5th Mahrattas. Lieutenant Heinz Werner Schmidt, Rommel's personal aide, described a crucial moment in the battle on 21 June:

'For a moment an unexpected minefield delayed our advance. Then the Panzers broke through, with the infantry and the anti-tank guns behind them. The Indians, particularly the 2/5 Mahrattas, hit back as best they could. But they seemed to have been stunned by the suddenness of the attack and the shock of the Stuka bombing. The 2/7 Gurkhas came racing up in Bren-carriers to counter-attack. But they were swept down, swept aside, swept back by the concentrated fire of machine guns, anti-tank guns and mortars'. (*With Rommel in the Desert*, Harrap, London 1951).

This action provides a classic example of the use of Carriers as light tanks in circumstances born of desperation, with disastrous consequences. With no overhead protection and only light armour elsewhere, the vehicles were particularly vulnerable to shrapnel from artillery airbursts and the guns of strafing aircraft.

North-West Europe

The role of the Universal Carrier in the liberation of the occupied countries of North-West Europe following the allied landings in Normandy on 6 June 1944 (Operation Overlord), where the primary task of the carrier platoons was to provide support to the mortar platoons and medium machine gun platoons of each battalion, has often been overlooked. Yet during the allied breakout from the beachheads the carrier platoons were constantly in action, probing forward to attack enemy positions and suffering serious losses in the process. Once this initial task had been taken over by more heavily armoured fighting vehicles, the carriers ran what amounted to a shuttle service between the beachheads and the forward positions, transporting everything from replacement troops and munitions to urns of tea. As allied forces advanced deeper into enemy territory, Universal Carriers, scouting ahead of the main columns, were often the first to make contact with the inhabitants of towns and villages from which the Germans had retreated.

In the weeks following Operation Overlord a number of airborne operations were planned, culminating in Operation Market Garden, the partially successful attempt to seize several key bridges that

ended in disaster for the British 1st Airborne Division at Arnhem. To support these operations, a number of Universal Carriers were modified to Universal Carrier

Top: A Bren Carrier manned by Free French soldiers in action during the campaign in Syria, June 1941. (ECP Armees)

Above: Panzer IV tanks roll past a knocked-out Scout Carrier during the Western Desert campaign. Some may argue this is a Universal Carrier. (Bundesarchiv)

Left: New Zealand soldiers and their Scout Carrier in Tunisia, May 1943. The soldier on the left appears to be wearing an Afrika Korps cap. If the entire rear of the driver's side of the carrier is not visible it is ifficult to tell the difference between a Scout Carrier and a Universal Carrier. (Australian War Memorial)

Right: The crew of a New Zealand Bren Carrier having a 'brew up' in the North African desert.

Below: Universal Carriers coming ashore at Salerno, Italy, in September 1943. (Via John McKenna)

Bottom: A Medium Machine Carrier version of the Universal Carrier. (The Vickers MG is not an expedient add-on here but rather part of the factory stowage design) of the Saskatoon Light Infantry in Italy, March 1944. (Canadian Army Museum)

No 1 Mk III (Airborne Configuration) specification, which involved the removal of all unnecessary weighty material, including some armour plate, and the addition of a mounting for a three-inch mortar on the rear structure. The intention was to airlift the modified carriers using the massive General Aircraft Hamilcar transport glider, which could also carry light tanks such as the Tetrarch.

Scout Carriers of the Guards Armoured Division passing through an English village on manoeuvres in 1939. (IWM)

The people of Aalst, Belgium, turn out to welcome men of the Irish Guards and their Universal Carriers. (Robert Jackson Collection)

Left: British soldiers showing off their carrier to a couple of admirers in Egypt, 1945. (Via John McKenna)

Below: Universal Carriers leading a British column on the approach to the River Orne, June 1944. Gliders of the 6th Airborne Division can be seen in the background. (Robert Jackson Collection)

This Ford Universal Carrier, pictured at a re-enactment function, bears the insignia of the 43rd (Wessex) Division, which was a formation of the 21st Army Group. (Wikimedia Commons)

Above: A Universal Carrier Mk I fitted with an experimental armoured hood. (Via J.R. Cavanagh)

Right: A column of Loyd Carriers. The rear-most vehicle is towing a 6-pounder anti-tank gun, a weapon that entered service in May 1942 after numerous production delays. (Via J.R. Cavanagh)

The Universal Carrier Mk I with the deep wading kit installed. The Irish Guards at Aalst, 18 September 1944. (Robert Jackson Collection)

A Universal Carrier Mk II showing the mud guards with integral steps and the relocated headlight. (Robert Jackson Collection)

Carriers were widely used for casualty evacuation: British casualties await transport back to the beachhead in Normandy, July 1944. A Sherman tank is in the background. (Robert Jackson Collection)

Universal Carrier 43rd Wessex Division, British XXX Corps advance through North-West Europe. Note the deep wading kit mounting pads welded around their upper hulls. (Robert Jackson Collection)

The crew of a Universal Carrier is welcomed by Belgian civilians during the liberation of Tournai. (Robert Jackson Collection)

Universal Carrier with deep wading kit enters a newly liberated village in Holland. (Robert Jackson Collection)

Left: A Universal Carrier Mk II, with the front portion of the mud guard removed leaving behind the crew step, seen during the bitter fighting in North-West Europe, late 1944. It also has the deep wading kit mounts. (Robert Jackson Collection)

Centre: Men of the Netherlands Motorized Infantry Brigade in their Universal Carrier. They were involved in bitter combat with Dutch Waffen SS troops during the advance to Arnhem in September 1944. (Robert Jackson Collection)

Below left: With a Universal Carrier in support, British soldiers march into a Dutch town. (Robert Jackson Collection)

Below right: A Universal Carrier knocked out during the Battle of Arnhem, September 1944. (Robert Jackson Collection)

A casualty of the 49th (West Riding) Division is carried to a Universal Carrier during Operation Market Garden, September 1944. This photograph shows the tubular guards of the Mk II welded along the top edges of the armored hull, the deep wading mounting pads, and the rear towing hook mount. (Robert Jackson Collection)

British troops with Loyd Carrier owing a 6-pdr anti-tank gun in Germany. (Robert Jackson Collection)

A Universal Carrier and Hamilcar glider seen during Operation Varsity. (Robert Jackson Collection)

The Eastern Front

Some 200 Universal Carriers were delivered to the Soviet Union from British and Canadian stocks between June 1941 and the end of the year. Further deliveries brought the total to 2,560 Universal Carriers and Loyd Carriers by the end of the war in Europe.

Rigt: Men of the Regina Rifle Regiment and their Universal Carriers. The Regiment landed in Normandy on 6 June 1944 as part of the 7th Infantry Brigade, 3rd Canadian Infantry Division, and fought in North-West Europe until the end of the war. (Canadian Army Museum)

Above left: This Lend-Lease Universal Carrier Mk I in Soviet service appears to have emerged second best from an accidental encounter with a Polish Army IS-2 main battle tank.

Above right: Soviet soldiers passing through Bucharest, Romania, in a Lend-Lease Universal Carrier Mk I.

Left: A Soviet Lend-Lease Universal Carrier Mk I on reconnaissance on the Eastern Front.

The Far East

The campaign in Burma, which began in 1942, when British and Empire forces were defeated by the Japanese and forced into the longest retreat ever experienced by the British Army, was hampered in the beginning by shortages of every kind. General (later Field Marshal Viscount) William Slim, commanding the Burma Corps, which was subsequently expanded to become the Fourteenth Army, wrote in his memoirs that 'I was horrified at (the 1st Burma Division's) low scale of equipment. It had never been up to even the standard of the 17th Division in this respect – the whole division, for instance, could only muster one improvised carrier platoon, instead of one per battalion.'

The problems confronting the British commanders in Burma were compounded by the demands of other theatres. For example, the 17th Indian Division, mentioned above, hurriedly assembled from other formations, had been trained and equipped, like all other Indian units, for desert warfare in the Middle East, and it was soon apparent that its transport, which was entirely mechanical and which included many Universal Carriers, was incapable of operating off-road except in open country. Another major problem was that troops and equipment intended to strengthen the allied forces in Burma were diverted to defend Singapore, under attack by Japanese forces which had advanced down the Malay Peninsula. In the end it proved to be a useless exercise,

The terrain in Burma was not conducive to off-road operations, as this image of a badly bogged-down vehicle shows. (Australian War Memorial)

A Universal Carrier Mk I, with a field-expedient flotation fixture for river crossing. The fuel drums are empty and provide the buoyancy, possibly taken during the Burma campaign in 1945. (Australian War Memorial)

.as the Singapore garrison surrendered in late February 1942. An unknown number of Universal Carriers were among the equipment sent to Singapore, and a few saw brief action with the 4th Battalion the Suffolk Regiment on 11 February. Others were used by the 2/18th Australian Infantry Battalion Carrier Platoon in an attack on Japanese positions at Bukit Timah village.

About forty Universal Carriers were used by American forces in the Philippines at the time of the Japanese invasion in 1942, these being part of a cargo of 57 vehicles from a transport vessel that had become stranded in Manila harbour while en route to Hong Kong, where the carriers had been intended to equip two Canadian motorized battalions. The Americans soon learned to their cost how vulnerable the exposed carrier crews were to intense small arms fire. Australian carrier crews experienced similar problems in New Guinea, as one account in the New South Wales Lancers Memorial webpage explains:

'On 23rd November 1942, General Clowes at Milne Bay, New Guinea ordered a small number of Bren Gun Carriers to Cape Endaiadere as direct support to American troops operating in this area. It was made clear to the Americans that the Carriers were too lightly armoured and the crews too exposed for them to be used as tanks. In addition, they lacked any overhead protection from sniper fire, shell splinters and were extremely vulnerable to flank attacks. Thus they were forced to work with infantry support.

'The aftermath of an attack at Cape Endaiadere on 5th December, resulted in vehicle crews being roughly handled and resulted in the abandonment of five vehicles. The supporting American infantry found they could not advance any further and the attack was called off. Sadly, it proved yet again, the futility of attempting to use inappropriate vehicles as tanks'.

Returning to Burma, carriers were used whenever possible to push out patrols in search of the elusive enemy, but it was in the defensive battles of Kohima and Imphal later in the campaign that they really came into their own, providing rapid transport of troops and supplies to defensive outposts around the besieged perimeters. Some were also used by units of the Royal Air Force Regiment; among other tasks, they ferried short-range radar sets, landed at Imphal's airstrip by C-47 aircraft, to the positions where they were to be installed.

Two separate actions during the Burma campaign involving Universal Carriers resulted in an NCO of the Indian Army being awarded the Victoria Cross. He was 28-year-old Havildar (Sergeant) Parkash Singh, serving in the Bren Gun Carrier Platoon of 5th Battalion, 8th Punjab Regiment, which was engaged in stiff fighting on the Mayu Peninsula in the

Arakan. On 6 January 1943, the platoon was attacked by a strong Japanese patrol near Donbaik and the platoon commander was wounded. Unable to continue, he handed over command to Parkash Singh, who noticed two other carriers bogged down in a nullah, a watercourse running through a steep narrow valley. Parkash Singh drove to within hailing distance of the bogged carriers, shouting to their crews to abandon their vehicles and run for cover while he provided covering fire. Then, his own Bren gunner being wounded, he charged towards the enemy, firing the Bren himself while driving with the other hand. Having driven the enemy out of their positions, he returned under heavy fire and rescued the crews of the stranded carriers, bringing all eight men to safety.

On 19 January, the battalion carriers again came under heavy anti-tank fire in the same area, and several of them were destroyed including that of the Platoon Commander. The crews of the destroyed vehicles were given up for dead, and the rest of the carriers withdrew, but Parkash Singh wanted to establish for certain if there were any survivors among the burning wrecks. Driving down the beach under intense enemy fire, he found an officer and his driver in their badly damaged carrier. The men were too badly injured to be moved, so Parkash Singh rigged a makeshift tow chain and towed their vehicle to safety, exposed to enemy fire all the while. For his selfless bravery Parkash Singh was awarded the Victoria Cross, although the original recommendation specified the Victoria Cross and Bar.

Singh rose to the rank of Major in the post-independence Indian Army. He died in 1991, aged 77, while undergoing heart surgery in London.

The Universal Carrier Post-War

The Universal Carrier, despite its obvious limitations when used to undertake tasks to which it was unsuited, served the Allies well until the end of the war in the Pacific, and many were deployed with the Australian and New Zealand forces that formed the Allied Forces of Occupation in Japan in the immediate post-war years. They also served with the British Commonwealth forces in Korea from 1950 to 1953, and in 1956 the Egyptian Army used them against Israel forces during the campaign in Sinai.

About 300 T-16 carriers were supplied to Argentina by the United States after the Second World War, 180 being supplied to the army, 90 to the navy and others to militia and police forces. Some were also used as test vehicles for various types of ordnance.

The army of the Republic of Ireland received over 200 Universal Carriers during the war years, and some may have been used by the Irish Army during United Nations peacekeeping operations in the Belgian Congo in the early 1960s. Some carriers

Australian Universal Carriers crossing a pontoon bridge during the Korean War. (Korean War Veterans Association Australia)

In the British and Commonwealth armies, it was the Ferret scout car, seen here on patrol in Cyprus, that mosly replaced the Universal Carrier.

The Ferret Armoured Car, also commonly called the Ferret Scout Car, was developed by Daimler as a result of a British Army requirement issued in 1947. It followed other very successful wheeled light reconnaissance vehicles built by Daimler during the Second World War. It was intended to replace the Daimler Reconnaissance Scout Car, but also proved a more than adequate replacement for the Universal Carrier, having excellent off-road performance. Like the carrier, it carried a three-man crew and the Mk I (seen here) had an open top, but subsequent models were fitted with a small turret mounting a machine gun.

supplied to the Netherlands were certainly used during the immediate post-war years in the colonial struggle between Dutch forces and Indonesian revolutionaries.

Contemporary Light Tracked Vehicles

A Carden Loyd Tankette Mk VI displayed in a Swedish museum.

Above: TK-3 Tankette in the Polish Army Museum.

Right: Polish TK-3 Tankette in Czechoslovakia.

Carden Loyd Tankette Mk VI (Britain)

A cross between a light tank and a machine gun carrier, the Carden-Loyd Tankette was a huge success on the export market, being cheap to purchase and reproduce. Although sometimes classed as light tanks, the Carden-Loyd series of AFVs were intended at the outset to be machine gun carriers. The whole purpose of the Tankette was the rapid deployment of troops armed with machine guns, which were not intended to be fired from the vehicle itself, although a tripod mounting for a machine gun was attached to the front of the hull. The Tankettes could also be used to tow light howitzers. The first was the Mk IV, started as a private venture by Major G. Le Q. Martel and subsequently manufactured by Vickers for the home market and the world export market. Production began in 1927.

TK-3 Tankette (Poland)

In 1929 Poland purchased a single Carden Loyd Mk VI Tankette and subsequently ordered ten more, together with spare parts. The British design was progressively modified by Polish engineers and manufactured as the TK-1 and TK-2. In 1930 a heavier and much improved variant, the TK-3, was produced, and entered service with the Polish Army in 1931. About 300 TK-3s were produced by the PZI (National Engineering Works) at Ursus, near Warsaw. The Tankettes formed the main body of the Polish Army's armoured force at the outbreak of the Second World War, and although they were no match for the German armour of the time they were ideal for reconnaissance and infantry support, their small size and low profile making them difficult targets. The TK-3s suffered heavy losses during the German invasion of Poland in September 1939. About 24 were fitted with a 20mm cannon just before the outbreak of hostilities, and these were much better placed to engage the lighter types of German armoured vehicle than those armed with a single machine gun.

T-27 Tankette (USSR)

Based in the Carden-Loyd Mk VI, which was produced under licence in the USSR, the T-27 was developed during the 1930s and featured a larger hull than the original British design, with an improved running gear and a mounting for a Soviet 7.62mm DT machine gun. The T-27 entered service in February 1931 and during its useful life with the Red Army it was used mainly as a reconnaissance vehicle. The T-27 was air-transportable, the concept being proven in the mid-1930s when the AFV was airlifted over considerable distances slung under a Tupolev TB-3 bomber/transport. The T-27 was widely used in the troubled 1930s to help put down local rebellions in the central republics of the USSR. Some were still in service in 1941, and it is known that a few took part in the defence of Moscow. Quite a number of T-27s were also used for experimental purposes, being fitted with flamethrowers and recoilless cannon. The T-27, which had a very cramped interior, was not popular with its crews.

CKD/PRAGA T-33 Tankette (Czechoslovakia)

In the 1920s, the government of the newly-created independent state of Czechoslovakia realised that if their embryo nation was to survive, it would need to build up a thriving and modern armaments industry. This it succeeded in doing with remarkable speed, the Skoda company of Pilsen, in particular, quickly becoming world-renowned for the quality of the weapons it produced. In 1927, the CKD (Ceskomoravska Kolben Danek) Company was formed by the amalgamation of four tank-manufacturing firms, and this enterprise set about manufacturing a tankette called the T-33, which like many others of its type was based on the British Carden-Loyd Mark VI, some examples of which had been obtained by the Czechs. Crews who tested the T-33 reported that they did not like it, but it went into production for the Czech Army anyway. Seized by the Germans in 1939, many CKD Tankettes were used in action on the Eastern Front in 1941. In fact, about one-quarter of the armoured fighting vehicles used by the Germans in 1940-41 were of Czech origin.

Carro Veloce CV 33 Tankette (Italy)

From 1933, a new generation of fast, lightly armoured tanks was developed by the Ansaldo Armaments and Heavy Industry Company for the Italian Army. The first of these was the Carro Veloce (Fast Tank) CV 33, which yet again was an improved version of the Vickers Carden Loyd Mark VI. Designated L3/33 in military service, the CV 33 and a developed version, the CV 35 (L3/35) saw operational service in Abyssinia (Ethiopia) in 1935 and in the Spanish Civil War, where an Italian armoured force was virtually wiped out at Guadalajara by far superior Russian-built

A Russian T-27 on display at the Park Patriot Museum in Moscow, formerly the Kubinka Tank Museum.

The T-33 Czechoslovak-designed Tankette with its distinct cream, brown and green camouflage pattern.

Carro Veloce CV 33 Tankette on display at the Bovington Tank Museum, UK and lined-up on the battle field with crew.

Russian T-37A Light Tank on display at the Park Patriot Museum, Moscow, formerly the Kublinka Tank Museum.

A Japanese Type 94 Tankette on display at the Australian War Memorial.

trials and found to be unsatisfactory. After substantial redesign, the vehicle emerged as the T-37, which entered production in 1933 and which incorporated several major improvements such as a suspension based on that of the French AMR 33 light tank. Production continued until 1936, the T-37 being built in several versions. Despite the fact that it was obsolescent the T-37 was used in combat during the early stages of Operation Barbarossa in 1941.

Type 94 Tankette (Japan)
The Japanese Type 94 Tankette was yet another small fighting vehicle based on the Carden-Loyd Mark VI. It was intended for light reconnaissance and patrol duties, and also for towing ammunition and supply trailers. As the vehicle was intended for operation in hot climates, it was provided with asbestos insulation to protect the occupants, of whom there were two: the driver seated to the right of the front-mounted engine, and the commander standing ehind him inside the small turret. This was unpowered, and to traverse it the commander had to push his shoulder against the machine gun. A company of Type 94s, usually consisting of six vehicles towing tracked trailers, was assigned to each Japanese infantry division. More than 800 Type 94s were manufactured and further development led directly to the Type 97 light tank. The Type 94 was used in all Japan's campaigns from 1934 onward, and surviving vehicles were still in use at the final surrender in 1945. Many are still to be found in tank museums all around the world.

T-26s. After the Axis invasion of the Balkans in 1941 some numbers of CV 33s and CV 35s were deployed to Yugoslavia for anti-partisan duties, some being captured by partisans and used against their former owners.

T-37 (USSR)
The inspiration for the T-37 light amphibious reconnaissance vehicle was Britain's Carden-Loyd AE 11 amphibious tankette, several of which were purchased by the USSR in 1931. The T-37 was not a copy of the British vehicle, which the Russians used as the basis for a much-developed version. This resulted in the T-33, which was subjected to numerous